MURDER AT GOLGOTHA

ALSO BY IAN WILSON

The Shroud of Turin

All in the Mind

Jesus: The Evidence

Exodus: The True Story

The Mysterious Shroud (with Vernon Miller)

The After Death Experience

Shakespeare:
The Evidence—Unlocking the Mysteries
of the Man and his Work

The Blood and the Shroud:
The Passionate Controversy Still Enflaming the World's Most Famous
Carbon-Dating Test

The Bible Is History

The Turin Shroud: The Illustrated Evidence

Before the Flood:
The Biblical Flood as a Real Event and
How It Changed the Course of Civilization

Nostradamus: The Evidence

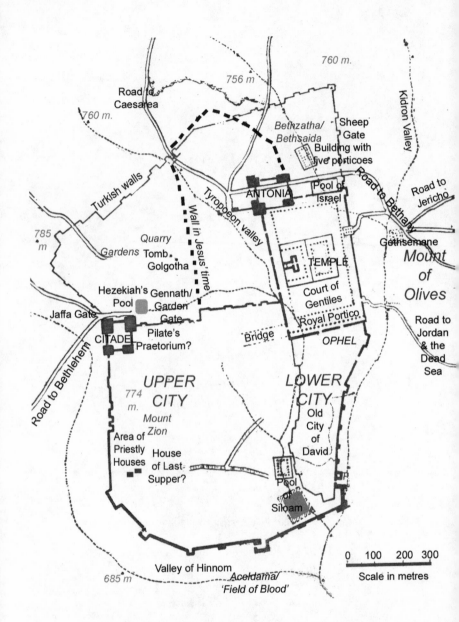

1—The city of Jerusalem, first century A.D., showing the main land-marks as they existed at the time of Jesus' crucifixion. These were changed beyond recognition less than half a century after Jesus' death.

MURDER
AT GOLGOTHA

Revisting the Most Famous
Crime Scene in History

Ian Wilson

St. Martin's Press
New York

www.stmartins.com

Library of Congress Cataloging-in-Publication Data

Wilson, Ian, 1941–
    Murder at Golgotha : revisiting the most famous crime scene in history /
Ian Wilson.—1st ed.
        p. cm
    Includes bibliographical references.
    ISBN 0-312-34932-7
    EAN 978-0-312-34932-5
    1. Jesus Christ—Trial.   2. Jesus Christ—Crucifixion.   3. Jesus Christ—
Resurrection.   I. Title.

BT450.W55 2006
232.96—dc22   2005043696
                        First Edition: April 2006

                10   9   8   7   6   5   4   3   2   1

Contents

✛

Contents

Acknowledgments

✠

As explained in the Introduction, the inspiration for this book owes much to my reactions on viewing of Mel Gibson's so pioneering, yet so flawed, movie, *The Passion of the Christ,* and also to my wife Judith's strong determination that those reactions should achieve printed form. My active personal interest in the events surrounding Jesus' death began in 1955 with an article by the British World War II hero Group Captain Leonard Cheshire, V.C. During the half century that has followed I have greatly valued innumerable insights from physicians, forensic specialists, clergy (both Roman Catholic and Protestant), archaeologists, papyrologists, experts in Jewish lore, and many others. The British physician Dr. David Willis, who died in 1976, was one of the first such helpers, and I have used as part of illustration 16 his anatomical reconstruction of Dr. Anthony Sava's hypothesis showing how a lance-thrust to the chest would have produced an outpouring of blood and "water." The New York medical examiner Dr. Frederick Zugibe has been another valuable consultant during the last two decades, although he would not necessarily support all the reconstructions suggested in this book. The *Jerusalem Bible,* published by Doubleday of New York, I have long regarded as a particularly fine translation of the Old and New Testaments into modern-day English, and this has been duly drawn upon for the Biblical quotations used here, though with occasional modifications wherever a particular word meaning needs highlighting. In the case of the book's illustrations the reconstructions of the pose of Jesus' shroud-wrapped body (illustrations 18 and 19) derive from experiments conducted in 2000 in association with the Los Angeles artist Dame Isabel Piczek. My wife, Judith, was the photographer both on that occasion and during later work attempting to reconstruct the scourging (illustration 10) and crucifixion (illustrations 14 to 16). The manuscript page featured in illustration 3 is from manuscript P66 in the Bodmer collection Switzerland, as reproduced in Victor Martin's *Papyrus Bodmer II* (Evangile de Jean chap. 1–14) Bibliotheca Bodmeriana, Supplement, 1962. The ossuary of Caiaphas featured in illustration 8 has been drawn by the author after a photograph by Garo Nalbandian. The reconstruction of crowning with thorns in illustration 11 is by the author and by Judith Wilson, though with use of anatomical detail of veins of the scalp drawn from Frederick Zugibe's *The Crucifixion of Jesus*, p. 35, after Sobotta's *Atlas of Descriptive Anatomy*, Urban and Schwartzenberg, Munich, West Germany. The reconstruction of the High Priest's costume is a drawing by the author with inspiration from a reconstruction initiated by the late Alfred Rubens in his excellent *History of Jewish Costume*. The details from the bones of Jehohanan in illustrations 14 and 15 derive from photographs by Mrs. E. A. Salomon, courtesy of the *Israel Exploration Journal*. Details from the Turin Shroud are variously after G. Enrie's photographs of 1931, Barrie Schwortz's of 1978, and fresh photography under the auspices of the Archdiocese of Turin in 2002. I am extremely grateful to George Witte of St. Martin's Press for his backing of this project, and to the editor, Nichole Argyres, for her care, patience, and excellent communications throughout.

Introduction

✠

The idea for this book was born after my husband Ian saw the Mel Gibson movie *The Passion of the Christ*. Maybe you too saw the film, along with the many millions of others around Easter 2004. Or maybe you heard the reports about the film's violence, and decided there was no way you were going to sit through that amount of cruelty.

Whatever your viewpoint, the chances are that quite a number who went to see the movie probably only had the vaguest idea of the events dramatized and went out of simple curiosity. The one certainty is that almost all who did, believers and nonbelievers alike, came out totally shell-shocked by the violence and inhumanity they had just seen. Very likely also, many had little idea how much of the events portrayed had been fact and how much fiction.

Like it or loathe it, Mel Gibson's movie certainly raised the awareness of things religious, especially in his two home countries, his former home Australia, and his present home, the United States of America. Certainly in Australia, as in the United Kingdom, the phasing-out of religious education in schools has led to generations of under-forties possessing only the sketchiest idea of the Christian story and the crucifixion. It is now fashionable to knock anything vaguely religious, and the proliferation of legal actions against members of the clergy has simply fuelled the trend towards the anti-religious in all forms of the media. The religious scene in the United States has been likened to "a pitched battlefield," largely as a reaction to the Gibson film. So be it.

Some of the most popular recent television series have been those put out under the Crime Scene Investigation umbrella. For example, *CSI: Miami* and *CSI: New York* are watched every week by literally millions of viewers not only in the United States, but also in other English-speaking countries. Individual episodes are generally well-crafted, frequently demanding close attention from the viewer to follow the various twists and turns as the crime is solved. There is a high reliance on forensic science as the glamorous stars examine the body, the crime scene, and the motives for the crime. Hopefully, the perpetrator will be brought to justice by the end of the episode.

Occasionally, the body is missing, demanding even more detective work to establish the truth of the whole scenario. While in real life, crimes in which the body is never found all too often end up in the "unsolved" box, fictional TV dramas such as *Cold Case* serve to show how even seemingly long-forgotten crimes can sometimes be resurrected and the truth at long last discovered.

But who would have believed that a murder case nearly two thousand years old could ever become "hot" again, and still without a body? Yet that is certainly what has happened by the screening of Mel Gibson's blockbuster movie *The Passion of the Christ*. The body is certainly still missing. The witnesses are long dead, and the crime scene changed beyond all recognition. Nonetheless this was the most famous murder in all history. Various movie treatments over the past decades, including Mel Gibson's *Passion*, have given their own spin on the events, but can the truth be more clearly established?

Certainly it can be, and that is the purpose of this book (though without any special intent to be a critique of Mel Gibson). Our aim is to re-examine much the same sequence of events followed in his movie, and to see how historical evidence, archaeological evidence, medical evidence, the Shroud of Turin, and other relevant items can all help to lead us towards what really happened. And the *true* events, as much as we can determine them, take nothing away from the drama and the vividness of the story.

Because of other writing commitments, Ian dictated much of the content of this book during a glorious winter weekend in Queensland, Australia. I then transcribed the tapes, and using as much original narrative as possible, edited the tapes to produce a manuscript which Ian then lengthened and reworked to ensure that it presents as full and accurate a picture of the events as is possible, given our present-day knowledge.

The book has been written for the honest enquirer who may know nothing, a little, or even a lot, about the story of Jesus. Hopefully it will introduce the subject to those who would like to be a little better informed about the Passion and murder of Christ. Certainly it is now for you, the jury, to follow the steps of what really may have happened as the Passion is played before you.

—Judith Wilson

1

A Crime Scene
Gone Cold?

✠

NEARLY TWO THOUSAND YEARS AGO Jesus Christ
was murdered in full public view, during daylight hours, in
what was most likely the year A.D. 30. The crime scene
was a hill called Golgotha, the "Place of the Skull," just
outside the city of Jerusalem in the then Roman-occupied
province of Judaea.

In ways that no one could have anticipated at the time,
the murder would turn out to be the most famous in all
history. In the course of subsequent centuries it changed
the lives of millions of people on every continent of the
world. It inspired Michelangelo to sculpt his *Pieta*,
Leonardo to paint his *Last Supper*, and Handel to write
his *Messiah*. In ways that Jesus could never have wanted,
it also led to the persecution of Jews, to Christians killing
fellow Christians over doctrinal differences, and to ongoing strife with the younger religion called Islam.

Jesus' murder would also become the most reenacted

in all history. Beginning with humble miracle plays back in the Middle Ages, such reenactments developed in our own time into highly developed dramatizations for cinema audiences. And never was any reenactment more dramatic and realistic than Mel Gibson's 2004 movie *The Passion of the Christ*.

I am still in a state of shock, having sat through two hours of almost uninterrupted, gratuitous brutality." "Graphic beyond belief . . . How anyone will be able to sit through this thing is the real mystery." "The film is unrelentingly violent. It's blood-soaked. Jesus gets so whipped you can see his ribs, blood spatters all over the cobblestones, and the sound is frighteningly realistic. And it doesn't stop after a pivotal scene or two—it goes on and on and on.

These are just a small sample of reviewer reactions to a film whose maker intended it to be as true and accurate a re-creation of the original events as humanly possible, a re-creation "directed by the Holy Ghost."

But was Gibson's *The Passion of the Christ* truly divinely inspired? Was it the closest that we can ever get to a re-creation of the last hours leading up to the Golgotha crime scene?

Mel Gibson's chief inspiration, and the bloody imagery that caused such revulsion amongst cinema audiences, derived not from the Christian gospels or historical sources but from the mystic visions of an early nineteenth-century German nun, Anne Catherine Emmerich, as recorded by a poet, Clemens Brentano. And,

2—The German mystic nun Anne Catherine Emmerich (1774–1824). Did Mel Gibson place too much reliance on her visions—lurid and often historically suspect—for the filming of his blockbuster movie *The Passion of the Christ?*

very sadly for Gibson's otherwise brilliant achievement re-creating on celluloid what Emmerich "saw" in her mind, any critical evaluation of these visions reveals them as lurid, hyperimaginative fantasies typical of the type of personality psychologists define as "hysteric." They have no sound historical or medical foundation.

What makes this situation all the sadder, given the huge energy and investment that went into the Gibson movie, is that today more than at any time in history we have forensic technologies that can reveal so much of what truly happened. Gibson was actually offered such forensic expertise, but turned it down in favor of the Emmerich fiction. The fact is that, even after such a long time lapse, the Golgotha of around A.D. 30 has far from gone entirely cold as a crime scene. Written testimony, topographic data, medical expertise, forensic techniques, and archaeology can all shed some surprisingly strong light on what really happened.

Accordingly, a searching revisit to the original events is the prime purpose of this book. As if from the viewpoint of a crime scene investigator, we will be questioning and reexamining every assumption about the last hours of Jesus' life, likewise about the manner and aftermath of his death. We will be resifting the Christian gospels as "witness" statements for which passages of these may be genuinely firsthand, and which have come down to us at second- or thirdhand. We will be looking at what is known from outside the gospels of how the Romans conducted their executions by crucifixion, how they fastened the victims to their crosses, and how long these might endure such an ordeal. We will be considering the possible authenticity of the various claimed relics of Jesus, such as the wood of the cross, the "crime" notice affixed to his cross, and the sheet in which his dead body was wrapped after being taken down from the cross. No possibly relevant clue will be dismissed out of hand. Likewise, nothing normally taken for granted will pass without fresh questioning.

Some of the huge difficulties of such an undertaking should not be underestimated. Over the centuries since Jesus walked its streets, Jerusalem has been changed almost beyond recognition. Within forty years of Jesus' death Jews throughout Judaea revolted against Roman rule, and the Romans had the greatest difficulty resubjugating them. As punishment, when they retook Jerusalem they razed to platform level the magnificent Temple where Jesus had preached during the last week of his life. When two generations later the remnant of surviving Jews revolted a second time, the Romans destroyed much of the rest of the city. They purged it of its Jewish citizens, sending them scattering across the world, and rebuilt it to a completely new layout as an all-Roman city, Aelia Capitolina.

Subsequent captures by Arabic Moslems, by French Crusaders, and by Turkish Moslems all similarly contributed to a relentless cycle of rebuilding, destruction, and rebuilding once more. It has been estimated that Jerusalem has been conquered thirty-seven times since its foundation, with no less than eleven changes of its dominant religion since Jesus' time. Present-day Old City Jerusalem is a noisy, bewildering maze, partly covered over, its alleyways teeming with small shops and stalls. It abounds with guides for the very simple reason that even those who arrive in the city armed with guide books can rarely find their way to, or identify, the sites they may have travelled thousands of miles to see.

While at above-surface level, nearly all the Jerusalem buildings that Jesus might have known have long since disappeared during the last few decades, Israeli archaeologists have unearthed many of their buried remains. These findings will be helpful to our crime scene investigation. Whenever anyone wants to build a new house or office block in central Jerusalem, there is a near guarantee that digging down to foundation level will reveal long-buried ancient ruins. The Israeli government rightly insists on bringing in archaeologists whenever this occurs, and as a result of their endeavours, more has been discovered about the Jerusalem of Jesus' time during the last four decades than at any previous time in history.

And as well as possible archaeological evidence, written evidence from witnesses of the period survives. Very few events of ancient times have four, different, near-contemporary accounts of what occurred, yet that is certainly what we have in the form of the gospels ascribed to Matthew, Mark, Luke, and John. It is true that theological studies have long shown that these documents are not entirely the immediate, first-hand, eyewitness statements that we might wish for. Indeed, during the nineteenth century a whole clique of German Protestant theologians made quite an industry of representing these as written by people who had never known Jesus at first hand, and who had lived long after the events.

But the recent Israeli archaeological findings have been showing the writings to be of greater value as testimonies than many have given them credit for. For instance, ruins of the building with five porticoes, where Jesus is described as healing a paralyzed man, have come

3—Writing of the testimonies . . . Well-preserved despite its age, a page from a manuscript of the original Greek text of the gospel of John, found in Egypt during the last century and preserved in the Bodmer collection in Switzerland. Characteristics of the handwriting enable the manuscript to be dated to the late second century A.D., less than two centuries after Jesus' death. Highlighted is the word *Bethsaida,* a reference to the Jerusalem building with five porticoes that Jews knew as *Bethzatha.* This was destroyed shortly after Jesus' death and rediscovered by archaeologists only within recent decades.

to light during excavations. Referred to as "Bethzatha" in the John testimony (John 5:2), a number of clues show this to have been the very setting John mentions. This is but one of many indications that the gospels were written not long after Jesus' death, from the recorded reminiscences of (though not necessarily by) people who had been in Jerusalem with Jesus, who had attended his healings, who had listened to his preachings, and who knew how he was killed.

And while—even in the case of Roman emperors—we may often know details of these lives only from copies of lost original documents made by medieval scribes, Jesus is better documented in near-contemporary manuscripts. Experts can often accurately date manuscripts to within a couple of decades, using clues from the way handwriting and punctuation have changed over the centuries. In the case of the events of Jesus' life, manuscript scraps identifiable as from the Matthew and John testimonies have been found that are datable to within a century of Jesus' lifetime. Three fragments from a papyrus copy of the gospel of Matthew, found in Egypt at the end of the nineteenth century, and preserved in Magdalen College, Oxford, England, have been dated by German specialist Carsten Thiede to around A.D. 70. And a single scrap from a papyrus copy of the gospel of John, preserved in the John Rylands Library, Manchester, England, is generally accepted by scholars to date no later than the second century, and quite probably from about A.D. 120. From the crime scene investigation point of view, we may consider the gospels as testimonies—attestations by individuals with a good claim to be consulted for their insights on the original events—and this is how we will refer to them from now on.

It has also long been fashionable to pay no attention to any of the various so-called relics of Jesus—for example, certain scraps of wood which are supposed to be from his cross, nails which are supposed to have been driven through his hands and feet, the notice affixed to his cross describing him as "King of the Jews," and the Shroud in which he was wrapped after death.

This disregard is on the grounds that they are almost bound to be fakes, due to widespread forgery of such items in the Middle Ages. The great Reformation leader Martin Luther forcefully encouraged this dismissive attitude towards relics back in the sixteenth century. German theologians reinforced it during the nineteenth century, and it has prevailed until quite recently.

But now, thanks to the availability of evermore sophisticated forensic techniques, relics associated with Jesus' killing can be examined rather more dispassionately, and altogether more authoritatively, more than ever before. And as we will see, some turn out to have far greater credibility and evidential value than has previously been supposed.

The final issue that we will be addressing—one that inevitably raises the biggest questions of all—concerns what can have happened to the body of Jesus, so that it disappeared, seemingly without trace, less than two days after its burial? In the case of most investigations of a killing, there is at least a body that can be subjected to autopsy, and from which all sorts of clues can be drawn as to the circumstances of death. But in the case of Jesus the witness testimony is quite emphatic that his body vanished in some strange way from the tomb in which it had been laid while it was being closely guarded. The same witness testimony also speaks of him making appearances to the disciples in which he seemed to be very much alive, and—particularly puzzling—being seen eating solid food, yet also passing through solid, closed doors.

This is indeed some very strange stuff to be dealing with. And inevitably we should not expect to be able to come up with all the answers. Nevertheless, let the crime scene investigation begin. . . .

2

The Victim Profile

✠

IN ANY CRIME SCENE INVESTIGATION the case
file will generally have the victim's name written on its
front cover. So should the name on our victim's file be "Jesus Christ"?

The short answer is no. So commonly is "Jesus" used in
the English language, even as an expletive, that many suppose it to be the name that Jesus was actually called by
those who knew him. But this is forgetting that the language which Jesus, his parents, and his disciples spoke
between themselves was Aramaic, which was to Hebrew
as modern Italian is to classical Latin. To reflect this, Mel
Gibson set *The Passion of the Christ*'s dialogue partly in
Aramaic, and in the movie Jesus' disciples correctly address their master as "Yeshu." Because our testimonies
were written first in Greek, then in Latin, "Jesus" is simply the form these adopted from "Yeshu."

Similarly, "Christ" is simply the Greek word for "Messiah." In Hebrew this means the "anointed one," and it was the title that Jewish kings traditionally received after the ritual anointing that was the equivalent of their being crowned as king. Because the coming of a new Messiah/Christ was the Jewish people's great hope for freeing themselves from Roman rule, Jesus would never have openly advertised himself as Jesus "Messiah" or Jesus "Christ." Or, at least, not until he was fully prepared to take the consequences. To the people of his own time he would simply have been known as "Yeshu son of Joseph," after his father, or "Yeshu of Nazareth," after his hometown, this latter notably being the form that our testimonies preferred.

In any crime scene investigation, one important task is to build up a profile of the victim, because information about his social and psychological background can yield clues to the motives for someone wanting him killed. Though Jesus lived at a time before birth certificates, there is general agreement amongst the witness statements that his mother was named Mary. Three of the same four sources—the exception being John—name Mary's husband as Joseph, whose occupation according to Mark 13:55 was that of a carpenter. Despite Joseph's relatively humble status—also, two lengthy attestations that he was not Jesus' biological father—both the Matthew and Luke witness statements provide Jesus with an ancestral pedigree, via Joseph, stretching back to the royal dynasty of Israel founded by King David, and indeed beyond. So Jesus theoretically had some royal blood flowing through his veins, assuming that Joseph *did* play some part in his paternity.

Amidst such genetic uncertainties, can we at least be sure when Jesus was born? No, not exactly. According to the Matthew testimony, he was born during the reign of Herod the Great. But as Herod died in 4 B.C. after reigning well over thirty years, Jesus would have to have been at least four years old at the time that the official Christian calendar has him being born, in the year A.D. 1. The Christian calendar that we use today is in fact based on a number of miscalculations made by a sixth-century monk, Dionysius Exiguus, who took no account of when King Herod reigned. Dionysius fixed the day of Jesus' birth as December 25, a date that had earlier been chosen, not because it had any scriptural authority but because it conveniently coincided with a popular Roman holiday. And he calculated the year as A.D. 1, and not, as often supposed, A.D. 0, sometimes called "the year dot," which has never existed, except in popular imagination.

Inevitably, such confusions over the year and day when Jesus was born have implications for our trying to work out exactly how old he was when he died. But these simply cannot be helped, and nothing suspicious needs to be inferred from this lack of hard information. In antiquity, if an individual sprang into the limelight late in his life, only then to have that life tragically cut short, the memories of those who knew him concerning when, how, and where he was born could often be very vague. In such circumstances it was not uncommon for biographers to invent sometimes fanciful birth stories, as certainly occurred in the case of Egyptian pharaohs and Middle Eastern emperors.

And the silence about Jesus' birth in the Mark and

4—**Galilee and its fishing community,** the environment in which Jesus grew up and which features prominently in the four testimonies recording his life and teachings. [A] Part of the northern section of the Sea of Galilee, a very fertile region to this day. [B] Reconstruction of a fishing boat of Jesus' time discovered during a drought in 1986 and now preserved in Israel's Yigal Allon museum. Coins and pottery dated the boat to the first century A.D.

John testimonies—both of which would have been written as *the* accounts of Jesus' life and death for their individual, early Christian communities—may be rather more valuable than the apparent knowledge exhibited in the

Matthew and Luke versions. In these latter the birth stories are notably never alluded to again. Additionally note-
worthy is that the original Hebrew of the Old Testament
prophecies about the Messiah's coming carries no expec-
tations that this individual would be born by anything
other than normal means. Only when these prophecies
were translated into Greek for the benefit of Greek-
speaking Jews did the Greek word *parthenos* come to be
used for the young woman who would give birth to the
Christ. And as *parthenos* carries the specific meaning of
"virgin," so those communities rightly or wrongly came to
expect that the Christ/Messiah could only be from a
woman who was a virgin *intacta*.

We are on more certain ground concerning Jesus' district of origin. As all testimonies agree, this was Galilee,
a Roman province that lay well over a hundred miles
north of Jerusalem. In contrast to Jerusalem's surroundings, much of which are desert and semidesert adjoining
the lifeless, lethally saline Dead Sea, Galilee was altogether more fertile and agricultural in character. Its "Kin-
nereth' or Sea of Galilee teemed with fish, providing a
good source of income for resourceful fishermen. Its
population was comprised of predominantly country
folk, farmers, fishermen, and farm laborers. These spoke
with a strong Galilean accent, which to the sophisticated, urban Judaeans of Jerusalem made them sound
like country bumpkins. Jesus' teachings, with their allu-
sions to the size of a mustard seed, to the watering of
donkeys, to the nonfruiting of a fig tree, and to a hen
gathering her chicks under her wings (these within just a
single chapter), are full of imagery reflecting his upbring-

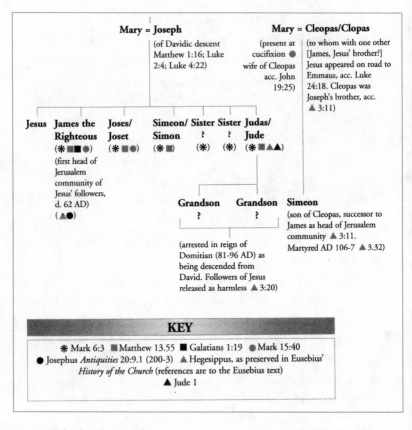

5—The family tree of Jesus, based on the assumption that the "brothers and sisters" listed in the Mark testimony (6:3), and mentioned elsewhere (John 7:2; Acts 1:14; I Corinthians 8:5) were Jesus' immediate family. Second-century Christian writers such as Tertullian and Hegesippus definitely viewed them in this way, even though they were also convinced of the divinity claimed of Jesus.

ing amongst such rustic people. And whereas the Judaean southerners were often inclined to collaborate with their Roman occupiers, recognizing their enjoyment of many commercial benefits from living under Roman rule, Galileans had a reputation for their being tiresome, boorish troublemakers.

What do we know about Jesus' immediate family members? Of his mother Mary our information is extremely limited. History has no way of determining whether Mary really was a virgin at the time of Jesus' birth, but the Mark witness statement and data from two early church historians, Tertullian and Hegesippus, indicate that she and Joseph subsequently had quite a large family. There seem to have been another four brothers, and at least two sisters. Some people, maintaining that Mary was always a virgin, insist that these people must have been cousins. But the four testimonies make clear enough that these were brothers and sisters in the normally accepted sense. There can also be little doubt that Mary was relatively young when she gave birth to Jesus. This is because the later testimony is firm and consistent that she was still alive at the time of Jesus' death, and actually present to witness this in all its horror. Joseph, on the other hand, is described as having been a widower before his marriage to Mary. And he is never mentioned in any context later than a time when Jesus was a twelve-year-old boy.

One brother of Jesus, James—known as James the Righteous, to distinguish him from the disciple of the same first name—stands out as an individual of some importance because he is mentioned in sources even outside the testimonies of Jesus' close supporters. Historical writers, such as Hegesippus and later Eusebius, make it clear that James was the first leader of the followers of Jesus who would stay on to promulgate Jesus' message in

Jerusalem, as distinct from carrying it elsewhere around the Roman Empire. And the well-respected Jewish historian Josephus, who lived just a generation after Jesus' murder, described how in A.D. 62 a Jerusalem High Priest had James killed with much the same ruthlessness as had been meted out to his brother three decades earlier.

Curiously, no surviving written testimonies describe what Jesus looked like. As an orthodox Jew he would probably have been bearded, for unlike the Romans, who were punctilious about being clean-shaven, this was not the case with the Jews. Probably his living amongst an agricultural community in which food was plentiful, as in Galilee, would have ensured that he would have been well built. Certainly he seems to have liked his food, because numerous episodes in the testimonies refer to him enjoying sometimes lavish meals accompanied by wine. In Mel Gibson's *Passion* Jesus was represented as a tall, handsome Caucasian to conform to mystic nun Anne Catherine Emmerich's vision:

> The complexion of our Lord was fair . . . and slightly tinted with red, but his exposure to the weather during the last three years had tanned him considerably. . . . His neck was rather long, with a well-set and finely proportioned head; his forehead large and high; his face oval; his hair, which was far from thick, was of a golden brown color, parted in the middle and falling over his shoulders; his beard was not any great length, but pointed and divided under the chin.

In actuality, whether Jesus was tall or short, bearded or clean-shaven, nothing in the written records provides us with authoritative information.

We are little better informed concerning how he dressed. Whereas his contemporary, John the Baptist, raised many an eyebrow by going around dressed only in animal skins, Jesus was certainly not of that mold. He is described as publicly reading from the scriptures and teaching in synagogues and the Jerusalem Temple, settings in which it was characteristic of Jews to take care to be seen wearing their Sabbath best. There was an occasion in which he was forcibly expelled from one of the former, but it was for what he said, not for any breach of the dress code. One of the clearest glimpses that we get of how he dressed would come at the very end of his life, when he was stripped of his garments immediately prior to his crucifixion. Clothes were expensive commodities in the ancient world, and one of the perks of his executioners was for their prisoner's clothing to be shared amongst them. According to the John gospel, Jesus' undergarment "was seamless, woven in one piece from neck to hem."

Whatever this garment actually looked like, it was sufficiently valuable that we are told his executioners decided to toss for it, rather than just cut it up between them. In his teachings Jesus would urge his listeners not to pay too much attention to how they dressed. However, there is never any suggestion that he was unkempt or slovenly.

What about clues from his childhood that this was someone who might, as an adult, turn out to be rather unusual? The Luke testimony embodies what may be a vestige of somebody's memory—very likely his mother Mary's—along these lines:

> Every year his parents used to go to Jerusalem for the feast of the Passover. When he was twelve years old they went up for the feast as usual. When the days of the feast were over and they set off home, the boy Jesus stayed behind in Jerusalem without his parents knowing it. They assumed he was somewhere in the party, and it was only after a day's journey that they went to look for him among their relations and acquaintances. When they failed to find him they went back to Jerusalem looking for him everywhere.
>
> It happened that three days later they found him in the Temple, sitting among the teachers listening to them, and asking them questions. And all those who heard him were astounded at his intelligence and his replies. They (his parents) were overcome when they saw him, and his mother said to him, "My child, why have you done this to us? See how worried your father and I have been, looking for you." He replied, "Why were you looking for me? Did you not know that I must be in my Father's house?" But they did not understand what he meant. (Luke 2:41–50)

This passage has been quoted in full partly because every parent can relate to and sympathize with such an incident occurring with their offspring. The child goes missing while the family is out shopping, or on an outing. Panic sets in. At first there is enormous relief when he is found safe and well. Then follows the reproach: "How could you have done this to us!" Whether Jesus was grounded or was punished afterwards is not recorded, but his reaction was definitely not that normally expected from a twelve-year-old. And hardly surprisingly, his parents had no idea what he meant by it.

But while this is the first recorded instance of Jesus exhibiting a mind of his own—and clearly a very questioning and unworldly one—it would be very far from his last. And it is surely ironic that it would be in this very same setting—the Jewish Temple—that Jesus would similarly question an authority rather higher than that of his parents, and with tragically fatal consequences.

3

Possible Murder Motives

✠

AFTER THE INCIDENT of the distraught parents losing then finding their son in the Temple, our four key testimonies have essentially no further details of our victim's life throughout the next two decades. Then, when according to the Luke testimony, the Roman Emperor Tiberius was "in the fifteenth year of his reign . . . Pontius Pilate was governor of Judaea . . . and . . . the high priesthood was held by Annas and Caiaphas" (Luke 3:1–2), a certain ill-dressed wild man began declaring the imminent coming of one who would open up the "Kingdom of God" for them. But to prepare themselves they first needed publicly to cleanse themselves of their worldly failings.

Living rough, and dressed only in animal skins, this "John the Baptist" performed these cleansings on the banks of the river Jordan, which runs southwards from Galilee to trickle into the Dead Sea some twenty miles to Jerusalem's east. And when Jesus—aged "about thirty" according to Luke 3:23—turned up amongst the thousands who heeded John's call, there seems to have been some kind of instant recognition between them, that he, Jesus, had to be the individual whom John had been proclaiming. And it was evident that whatever Jesus had been doing up to that point—presumably, quietly carrying on the late Joseph's carpentry business—he had acquired a very good working knowledge of the Jewish scriptures.

The journey to our victim's downfall was about to begin, for this little-known carpenter was becoming fired with a very strong sense of personal mission, and he began moving around the countryside talking about this to all who were prepared to listen to him. The group of followers that Jesus would gather around him were indeed a motley bunch in the eyes of the more traditional Jews, most of whom any worthwhile recruitment consultant would unhesitatingly have rejected as thoroughly unsuitable for helping him launch a religion to last for two thousand years and attract two billion adherents. After all, who in his right mind would even attempt to found a religion from a few commercial fishermen, a tax collector (in Jesus' time, notorious for their dishonesty), a couple of Greeks, a couple of ex-terrorists, and an avowed skeptic? And all of them possessing serious character flaws, with not a decent scholar or lawyer among them. When events later began to get tough, it was all too predictable that even this unlikely group's leader, the fisherman Simon, renamed by Jesus as Peter ("the Rock"), would break some solemn promises and repeatedly lie to save his own skin.

The message that Jesus was beginning to spread was

guaranteed to earn him enemies. For, as evident from the four testimonies, while Jesus recognized the traditional Jewish wisdom as set down in the old Hebrew Torah (today the "Old Testament" section of Christian Bibles), he had also acquired some "new," altogether less clear-cut lifestyle values which he said had come to him directly from God. According to him, while there was nothing fundamentally wrong with the Ten Commandments that the prophet Moses had taught, there were circumstances in life in which God looked for responses with a lot more "heart" or love to them. However normal and reasonable we might suppose our quest for the perennial desirables of health, wealth, status, and security, the excessive pursuit of any or all of these could positively block our ever enjoying one day that "Kingdom of God" that John the Baptist had proclaimed. Conversely, if only we could find more love in our hearts for those suffering from serious illnesses, for the poor, for the marginalized, and for those genuinely repentant because of their succumbing to some serious human weakness, then God and his unworldly Kingdom were ever at their closest amongst these. Such thinking seriously grated with the prouder amongst those who listened to this upstart carpenter.

To help convey his so simple yet so difficult-to-live-by message, Jesus crafted some highly original and memorable parables. Well over thirty of these have been recorded in three of the testimonies (that of John being the exception), and they show no signs of any garbling as from second-hand memories long grown dim. Rather, they have the quality of their having originated from a single, wry, and highly observant mind, and of their having been set down as near direct from that mind's lips as makes little difference.

Yet however simple Jesus tried to make his message, there were inevitably those who, quite aside from their finding it difficult to follow, seriously misunderstood what he had in mind. Even within Jesus' closest followers several seem to have thought that all his talk of some unworldly "Kingdom of God" was just so much smoke and mirrors. Their fervent hope was that his real mission was to lead them all in something practical: an armed revolt to expel the Romans and return Jewish territories to their true and rightful identity as God's own kingdom. Any reading between the lines of the four accounts of his "Miracle of the Loaves" shows that this was also high in the minds of the five thousand men who insisted on following him when he sought some peace out in the desert. According to the John testimony, after this army-size gathering had been fed:

> Jesus realized they were about to come and take
> him by force and make him king, [and] fled back to
> the hills alone. (John 6:15)

To attract such a following there has to have been something quite magnetic about our victim. It takes someone very special to walk up to a group of commercial fishermen and ask them to follow him, and then have them meekly do so, rather than tell him to take a jump in the lake. Something about him convinced people he

could look into their hearts. As the John testimony ex-
pressed it, he

> knew all people. . . . He never needed evidence about
> anyone. He could tell what someone had within.
> (John 2: 24–25)

But Jesus, who had no intentions of becoming any
kind of terrorist, would let down such supporters, individuals who would have steeled themselves to follow him in
an armed struggle against Rome's fearsome military
might. Amongst these followers Jesus' "turn the other
cheek" pacifism could only generate ill feeling. Additionally, he was hardly likely to win friends by reaching out to
people positively loathed by those same supporters. A
case in point was his agreeing to a Roman centurion's re-
quest to cure the paralysis afflicting his slave—a healing
recorded in the Matthew (8:5–13) and Luke (7:1–10) testimonies. Such helping of a Roman was tantamount to a
World War II Frenchman collaborating with one of
Hitler's Nazis. And it was made even worse by Jesus
warmly commending the centurion for the faith that he
had shown.

Similarly ill-suited to winning friends amongst more
mainstream Jewish society was Jesus' reported urging his
listeners to sell all their goods and give the proceeds to the
poor, while himself making no attempt to conceal his enjoyment of some liberal food and wine hospitality from individuals notorious for their loose morals. Though Jesus
justified himself by arguing that the "publicans and sin-

ners" providing him with this hospitality were most in need of the message that he brought them, those who were already trying to lead purer, less selfish lives could hardly be expected to view such double standards so kindly.

As a further point of friction, while upright Jewish society frowned upon any man associating with a woman outside his immediate family, Jesus clearly welcomed and enjoyed female company, and was rashly indiscriminate about strangers of this gender to whom he talked. As but one example, he made a special point of engaging in conversation with a woman who was drawing water from a well. She was a Samaritan, a group hated and despised by Judaeans and Galileans alike. Yet Jesus not only ignored such political considerations, he made such a favorable impression upon the woman, seeming to know many intimate details about her, that she returned to her village to relay what he had taught her with all the enthusiasm of a born-again disciple.

But though such seemingly unholy behavior was bound to foster resentment amongst both the straight-laced and the hotheaded, Jesus' preachings and healings in most other respects won him a very favorable reputation, even amongst the pro-Roman Judaean southerners. He reportedly attracted large crowds wherever he went. Several women whom he had healed, among these Mary of Magdala, a Galilean woman who had been suffering from some kind of psychiatric illness, had joined his traveling entourage. When at the last Passover time of his life he arrived on the outskirts of Jerusalem accompanied by these rather colorful women followers, together with his disciples, his mother, and her sister, he was certainly given the warmest of welcomes.

According to the Luke testimony he had asked one of his disciples to arrange for a donkey to be made available for what he clearly planned as a very special last entry into the city. This choice of such lowly transport was undoubtedly partly to appear humble rather than ostentatious. But it was also partly to make sure he conformed to what the Jewish scriptures foretold about how their Messiah would enter Jerusalem.

The surviving testimonies describe how, to the dismay of the ruling Romans, our victim was received by wildly enthusiastic crowds of people, waving palm branches, jostling each other for the best vantage position. The time of the Passover festival, when huge numbers of Jews traveled from far and wide to congregate on Jerusalem, was always a nervous one for the Roman authorities. From historical sources we know that Judaea's Roman governor Pontius Pilate was normally based at Caesarea on the Mediterranean coast. At Passover festival time, however, Pilate made a special point of staying in Jerusalem, just to be on hand in the event of any trouble. Despite the humble donkey that Jesus was riding, it is not difficult to imagine Pilate and his fellow Romans viewing with some unease the huge acclaim that this Jew was being accorded.

Neither would there have been much joy on the part of the Temple High Priest Caiaphas and his former High Priest father-in-law Annas, particularly if they had already heard something of Jesus' views on their running of the enterprise that he called his "Father's house." For the

Jerusalem Temple was theoretically the very centerpiece of the Jewish religion, the equivalent of the Kaaba at Mecca for today's Moslems, but architecturally altogether more showy. King Herod the Great had lavished a fortune on an ambitious rebuilding program to make it one of the Wonders of the World of its time. And every good Jew was expected to visit it at some time during his life to pray, and to offer up some form of livestock, to perform which sacrifice the Temple priesthood commanded exclusive rights. A rich man might offer up an ox, a middle-income individual a lamb, and a poor person something that might be as lowly as a pigeon. Temple priests would ritually slaughter these and burn them on the open-air altar on which two fires were kept constantly lit, with a third available as backup.

Every kind of creature suitable for sacrifice, together with the services associated with their offering, could be purchased in the Temple's precincts, but not with Roman money. This was because Roman coins bore images of Roman gods on them, and even any human likeness, such as the head of the emperor, was perceived as violating the second of the Ten Commandments. So the Temple priesthood minted their own imageless, "approved" coinage. And they had money changers set up at all key entry points to provide the necessary currency exchange, a transaction that accrued for them whatever profits they chose to set, with an extra margin for the changers.

High Priest Caiaphas was the man in charge of this operation. Dressed in his ceremonial finery he cut a highly impressive figure—a violet robe adorned with bells and tassels, a special mitre with a golden plate in front in-

6—Reconstruction of the ceremonial dress of Jerusalem's High Priest in Jesus' time, based on Biblical documentation and a very detailed description by the contemporary Jewish historian Josephus. Note the gold crown, the gold plate engraved with ancient Hebrew letters on his forehead, and the elaborate breastplate made up of twelve precious stones representing Israel's twelve tribes.

scribed "Holy to the Lord," and a breastplate with the names of the twelve tribes of Israel. His exalted status meant he had to keep himself pure from any contact with the dead or dying, even among his own relatives. He and his father-in-law Annas, whom he had succeeded in the office, were not so much holy men as functionaries running a commercial enterprise that was as thoroughly tuned to money-making as any Las Vegas casino. Their staff at the Temple—chief priests, lesser-ranking priests, scribes, animal carers, animal slaughterers, stokers, maintenance workers, security guards, stone masons, metal workers, money changers, and many more—ran into many thousands.

Caiaphas, Annas, and their fellow chief priests were not even chosen for any special piety. They and their fellow high-ranking colleagues belonged to a hereditary caste, the Sadducees, who handed different administrative posts down through their families from one generation to the next. The district of Jerusalem where they lived—one into which Jesus would be brought for interrogation the night he was killed—has been particularly well excavated by modern-day Israeli archaeologists. As a result of these excavations we know that the most senior priests lived a prosperous and comfortable lifestyle. Fine goblets have been found in their ruins, and the houses had elaborate mosaic courtyards. Because of their high position in society they had servants and guards in the manner of worldly princes.

All this commercialism in the name of religion was deeply offensive to Jesus, and it led to the only act of violence ever recorded on his part, one to be found in all four testimonies. Four days before the Passover festival he approached the Temple, within the precincts of which he had already been teaching daily. Seeing the serried rows of the money changers set up between the columns of the approach section, he knocked over their tables and set upon them with whips. According to the John testimony, he then released the animals and birds awaiting sacrifice with the words "Take all this out of here and stop turning my Father's house into a market."

Note again the words "my Father's house"—exactly those he had used to describe this very same building back when he had infuriated his parents by lingering in it as a twelve-year-old boy. This occasion has to have been even more volatile a scene—as dramatic in its impact as someone today knocking over all the gaming tables and switching off all the machines in a Las Vegas gambling casino. And it most certainly did not fail to come to the notice of the Temple's High Priest and his fellow Sadducean dignitaries. They could only perceive it as a direct assault on their business.

According to the Mark testimony, when they sent a small delegation to ask Jesus what authority he had for acting in this way, he deftly (and characteristically) deflected their question by asking one of his own.

"John's baptism, did it come from heaven, or from man?" (Mark 11:30). Though Jesus was not the first to use such a device, eighteen centuries before Sigmund Freud he was using the psychologist's trick of answering a question with a question. As he knew, they would be bound to avoid replying "man" because this would run contrary to John's huge, popular reputation for being directed by God. But if they answered "heaven," then Jesus could claim to have been acting with the same divine authority. Perceiving themselves caught between a rock and a hard place, the emissaries could only slink away mumbling that they did not know.

Inevitably, one option that the chief priests had was to arrest Jesus then and there as a troublemaker. Certainly they had sufficient security guards at their disposal at the Temple to do this. But such action risked being noticed by the large crowds daily gathering at the Temple during this Passover festival time. Many of these came specifically to hear Jesus talk about his "Kingdom," and they might well rush to his aid. This could spark off a wholesale riot, the last thing that they wanted happening on temple premises. The populace needed to be kept on their side at all costs. Anything else was bound to be bad for business.

So, while the John testimony is explicit that it was from Jesus' "cleansing of the Temple" action onward that the "chief priests . . . determined to kill him" (John 11:52), Caiaphas and his colleagues needed to look for some more covert means of arranging this. A means that preferably would turn the least possible spotlight on their involvement.

Meanwhile, were there any other groups who might have nurtured similarly hostile intentions towards Jesus? Well, yes, that very same passage in the John testimony mentions "the Pharisees" as also wanting Jesus killed. Additionally, our four testimonies are full of instances of Pharisees criticizing Jesus for his flagrantly flouting the strict letter of the laws that Moses had laid down. These include his disrespecting the Sabbath by conducting healings on that day, being too friendly to women, etc, etc. The Pharisees were a relatively new branch of the Jewish religion. They had founded the synagogues for preaching, for praying, and for listening to readings from the Torah, as they referred to what Christians call the Old Testament. And they actually shared Jesus' dislike for the way that the Sadducean priesthood were turning the Temple into a market. So, theoretically they should have been on Jesus' side, and after his death some would indeed defend Jesus' followers against the Sadducees (Acts 5:34). But while he was still alive they certainly ranked closer to his enemies than to his friends, constantly arguing with him over minor doctrinal differences.

Even so, from the ecstatic scenes that greeted Jesus on the last Sunday of his life, just five days before he would be put to death, it would have been difficult for any outsider to suspect the deep animosities that surrounded him. Nor could anyone—apart from the victim himself—have been expected to foresee the tragic events that were about to unfold. Yet, all too clearly documented in the surviving testimonies is that the countdown to one of history's most infamous and unjust killings had begun.

4

The Victim's Last Meal

✠

IN ANY INVESTIGATION of a murder, whether one that has been committed recently, or at some unknown time in the past, a fundamental task is to try to work out as accurately as possible some kind of timetable of the victim's last movements. Back in the time of Jesus our "Christian" calendar had, of course, not been invented. However, had even one of the authors of our key testimonies noted the year of the Roman emperor Tiberius' reign in which Jesus was killed, this could have saved generations of scholars and theologians umpteen hours of speculation.

As it is, the year that this event occurred actually carries the least certainty. According to the four testimonies, the High Priest at the time was called Caiaphas, and from consultation with historical sources we know that Joseph Caiaphas held the post from A.D. 18 to 37 in succession to his father-in-law Annas, who seems to have continued in office alongside him. This nineteen-year time frame can be narrowed to nine because historical sources make clear that the Roman governor Pilate, whom the testimonies describe as interviewing Jesus, was in charge of Judaea only between A.D. 27 and 36. And it can be narrowed even further, because the Luke testimony describes the Roman emperor Tiberius as having been in the fifteenth year of his reign—A.D. 29 of our present calendar—when John the Baptist began his public baptisms on the river Jordan. So, even if John had baptised Jesus very early, and Jesus spent only one year going about teaching and healing (most scholars think that it was three), there is a window of just six years, between A.D. 30 and A.D. 36, for the period in which Jesus' murder took place. Amongst scholars and theologians of all denominations A.D. 30 and 33 carry the most support for the likeliest years.

Seasonwise, the timing calculations reach altogether firmer ground. All the testimonies agree that the event took place just before the Jewish Passover festival, an annual commemoration of their ancestors' escape from slavery in Egypt that was, and still is, celebrated in springtime. Year by year the date for Passover is calculated by the paschal full moon, the extreme limits of which are between March 21 and April 25. (Because of the Christian Easter festival's relation to the Passover, its annual dates vary on exactly the same basis.) Likewise, the testimonies all agree that the day of the week on which Jesus was killed was the one before the Jewish Sabbath on Saturday, hence a Friday. And because the testimonies have reasonably abundant information about the events of the immediately preceding days, we can re-construct a brief calendar.

We know that our victim had spent some time during the nights immediately before and after his angry physical outburst in the Temple, in the village of Bethany—today a suburb of Jerusalem just a short bus ride along the road leading eastward to Jericho. In Bethany he was a hugely revered guest at the house of Lazarus, the man he had re-vived after he had apparently been dead and buried for three days. According to the John testimony, many Bethany villagers who had been present when this hap-pened, and who were thereby well-acquainted with the facts, were among those cheering the loudest when Jesus rode his donkey into Jerusalem (John 12:17). We know that Lazarus lived with his sisters Mary and Martha, and the very first night that Jesus arrived in their home Mary had welcomed him by bringing into the room a most ex-pensive and beautifully scented ointment. In full view of the disciples she then proceeded to rub this into Jesus' feet and wipe them with her hair, the whole house be-coming filled with the perfume that she had lavished.

This apparently innocuous act of grateful hospitality was to prove the final straw for one particular disciple, Ju-das Iscariot, one of the two of Jesus' followers who seems to have had some terrorist (that is, anti-Roman) back-ground. Judas' name, according to some interpretations, means "Dagger Man." As noted particularly in the John testimony, Judas roundly complained of the blatant ex-travagance he witnessed. "Why was this ointment not sold for three hundred denarii and the money given to the poor?" To which a nonplussed Jesus responded: "Leave her alone; let her keep it for the day of my burial. You have the poor with you always, you will not always have me" (John 12:5, 8).

Rather than his being moved by these words, Judas appears to have become determined from that moment on to help the Temple authorities capture Jesus in a behind-the-scenes, underhanded way. As the Matthew testimony reports in the immediate aftermath of Jesus' acceptance of Lazarus's sister's attentions, Judas

> went to the chief priests and said "What are you prepared to give me if I hand him over to you?" They paid him thirty silver pieces, and from then onwards he began to look for an opportunity to betray him. (Matthew 26:14–16)

That opportunity would not be long in coming.

On what would prove to be the very last evening of his life, Jesus chose to dine with the full complement of his disciples at a somewhat mysterious house in central Jerusalem—mysterious because the testimonies make it clear that the disciples had never been to this house before, and they had no idea who owned it. Two of the fishermen, Peter and John, were told to follow a man with a pitcher of water who would lead them to the house in question. There they were to ask the unnamed owner to show them to the "upper" or upstairs room that had clearly been prearranged for them. They would then take over all meal preparations in advance of Jesus and the rest of their party arriving—on this occasion, it would seem, without any of the women accompanying them.

So where was this house? Until comparatively recently the location of this "House of the Last Supper" has been supposedly irretrievably forgotten. Only within the last few years, however, has a very plausible theory developed that the site may have been that occupied by the definitely misnamed and mislocated "Tomb of David" in the hilly Mount Zion area just to the south of the old city wall. Lower stonework in this particular complex seems to incorporate blocks salvaged from Jerusalem's temple after its destruction in A.D. 70. During the two generations between this destruction and their "final" expulsion in 134 A.D., Jews were allowed back into the city, during which time these particular blocks seem to have been used to build a synagogue.

Was this a normal Jewish synagogue? Definitely not. The usual Jewish synagogues, wherever they were around the country, were always oriented towards the Temple. This particular example, even though the Temple lay only half a mile to its northeast, was instead orientated towards where Jesus' tomb is known to have been situated. It also had pious Christian graffiti scrawled on its walls. All the indications, therefore, are that this was a synagogue built and used by Jewish Christians who continued with Jewish-style religious observance (as specifically recorded of Jerusalem's first Christian community—see Acts 1:46), while venerating it as a place of very special Christian holiness. This is exactly how we might expect them to treat the site of one of the Christian faith's most seminal events. For it was at this very location on this most fateful of nights that Jesus told his followers that the bread and wine that he was offering them were his own flesh and blood. That very shortly this body and blood would be expended on their behalf. And that when this happened they, his very disciples, would scatter like sheep, but he would physically come back from death and actually precede them back to Galilee (Mark 14:28).

These solemnly delivered pronouncements were not the only cause for astonishment and disbelief sprung upon his guests by our victim that night. Surely mindful of their embarrassment when Mary of Bethany lavished attention on his feet, he performed exactly the same slavelike service for each of them. As described in the John testimony, he

> removed his outer garments, and taking a towel, wrapped it round his waist; he then poured water into a basin to wash the disciples' feet and to wipe them with the towel he was wearing. (John 13:5)

As he explained, this was an object lesson in the sincere humility that he expected from each of them:

> You call me Master and Lord . . . If I, then, the Lord and Master, have washed your feet, you must wash each other's feet. I have given you an example so that you may copy what I have done to you. (John 13:15)

Are we able to envisage the Last Supper scene that subsequently took place in that upstairs room that evening? The image that almost universally comes into everyone's minds is Leonardo da Vinci's famous, yet ruined, painting in Milan. In this painting the disciples are depicted seated at either side of Jesus at a long table, replete with tablecloth. Mel Gibson's *Passion* movie dramatised the scene in a similar manner. But is this actually how the dining room was set out? Probably not. According to the Luke testimony, the room in question was "furnished with couches." This immediately suggests the sort of banqueting couches long popularized by the ancient Greeks—though borrowed from nearby eastern cultures—on which guests would recline rather than sit up straight at a table. And such a seating arrangement readily explains the John testimony describing the disciple John, during this meal as "reclining next to Jesus," then "leaning back close to Jesus' chest." (John 13:21, 25).

We can be sure the day of the meal was a Thursday. But the testimonies differ frustratingly concerning whether the occasion being celebrated was a full Seder, the annual Jewish family get-together on which they ate unleavened bread the night before the actual day of Passover proper, or whether it was a more ordinary preliminary meal. According to the Matthew, Mark, and Luke versions of the story, it was the Seder meal, which would mean that Jesus' killing, which definitely took place the day following the Last Supper, occurred on Passover itself. While this undoubtedly makes for some beautiful "sacrificial lamb" symbolism, Jewish scholars convincingly insist this would be very unlikely historically, in view of so many Jewish religious sensitivities associated with the Passover day proper. Furthermore, the John testimony, which appears to be particularly strong with regard to the Passion Week events in Jerusalem, differs from the other three in being quite emphatic that the day of Passover was the day immediately after Jesus' killing, the Sabbath.

Whatever the true timing in relation to Passover, the events following the end of the meal have been clearly established. Judas was obviously unmoved by Jesus' demonstration of humility, and it was in the immediate aftermath of this occasion that he acted on his plan to help the High Priests arrest Jesus. He may have been helped by a simple matter of geography. He needed to find Caiaphas quickly, and a possible house where Caiaphas may have lived lay on the same Mount Zion hill, only a few yards from the very house in which we have theorized the Last Supper to have been held. Judas had only to slip away from the rest of the group, tell the High Priests that he knew where Jesus and his disciples would be sleeping overnight—a quiet, isolated spot where Jesus could be arrested with the least chance of resistance—lead a party of the Temple security guard to this place, identify which of the sleepers was Jesus, and then leave the rest to them.

Exactly as Judas expected, when Jesus and his disciples left the house of the Last Supper they strolled eastward along the line of the city walls, dropping down into the Kedron Valley before a short climb to some higher ground that everyone of the time knew as Gethsemane, literally, the "place of the olive press." Located on the Mount of Olives, en route between Jerusalem and Bethany, this has long been assumed to have been just a garden, one in which the disciples slept out in the open. And certainly Mel Gibson envisaged it as such in the very

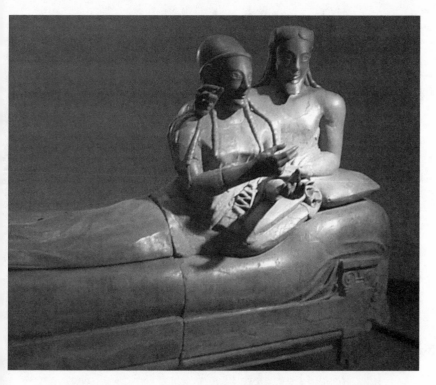

7—Is this how Jesus partook of the Last Supper? In contradiction of Leonardo da Vinci's famous painting of the Last Supper, which depicts Jesus and his disciples seated at a long table, the original Greek of the Luke testimony describes the room used by Jesus and his disciples as "furnished with couches." This indicates that Jesus and his disciples would have dined while reclining on such couches, which was a wide-spread custom among the peoples of the time. This is particularly clearly illustrated by the couple portrayed in the Etruscan statue (shown above), which is preserved in Rome.

haunting opening scene of his *Passion* movie. But was this scenario correct?

The difficulty for such an idea is that with the time of the year being around late March, and Jerusalem at an elevation of some twenty-five hundred feet, it would have been distinctly chilly for anyone to sleep overnight out in the open on cold, hard ground. The testimonies specifically mention fires being lit, even in the relatively sheltered courtyards of the High Priests' houses. And the testimonies make clear that the group that Jesus had brought to Jerusalem with him included his mother and her sister, women who can hardly have been younger than their fifties.

Thanks to some assiduous recent research by New Zealand scholar Joan Taylor, we now know that the real Gethsemane, while it included a garden, also included shelter in the form of a large cave that has been located some seventy yards north of what today the guidebooks still call the Garden of Gethsemane. This cave would have been a busy place every autumn, when olives were brought into it for pressing after being gathered from the surrounding groves. During the spring, however, well before the olives' ripening, it would have lain empty and idle. It would therefore have provided an ideal overnight shelter for Jesus and those accompanying him. Also, of course, an ideal place for him to be cornered and arrested with the least chance of escape.

We understand from the testimonies that Jesus did not immediately settle down in the cave for the night, but asked three of his disciples to stay awake with him outside in the garden while he prayed. Three times after his becoming absorbed in his own characteristically intense private prayers, he returned to find them fast asleep. He'd noticed earlier that Judas had slipped away, and clearly cognizant of the harrowing ordeal that awaited him, he could not hide his deep emotional distress.

So why was he so distressed? As he was deeply aware, the culmination of his whole mission as Messiah had come. He had to fulfill the prophecies by dying the most degrading and harrowing of deaths. The testimony of Luke, thought by many to derive from a physician, describes this "agony in the garden" manifesting in some overt physical symptoms:

> In his anguish he prayed even more earnestly, and his sweat fell to the ground like great drops of blood. (Luke 22:44)

Is there any way that a man could indeed "sweat blood"? According to the veteran New York medical examiner Frederick Zugibe, who has taken a great deal of interest in this description, Jesus was experiencing a classic "fight or flight" reaction. After a rush of adrenalin which would have caused his heart rate to increase, his blood vessels would have first constricted, and then dilated. This would have sent blood sugar levels soaring. He would have panted to increase his oxygen intake. This would have been followed by extreme physical tiredness, then exhausted resignation. His heart rate would have slowed, accompanied by sweating. As the blood rushed back into the capillaries close to the sweat glands these would have ruptured, generating great drops of sweat mixed with blood. Medically termed *haematodrosis*, this is readily recognizable as what Jesus was experiencing. So we have no reason to doubt the Luke testimony that "his sweat fell to the ground like great drops of blood."

As was soon evident in the arrival of Judas at the head

of a strong force of guards, "all with lanterns and torches and weapons" (John 18:3) sent by the Temple priests, there was nothing imaginary about Jesus' fears. Even at this late hour there must have been some accompanying senior Temple functionary for Jesus reportedly to have very pointedly remarked:

> Am I a bandit that you had to set out with swords and clubs? When I was among you in the Temple day after day you never made a move to lay hands on me. But this is your hour; this is the reign of darkness. (Luke 22:53)

Our victim made no attempt to resist arrest, and positively forbade his disciples from making any attempt to defend him. He was led meekly away.

Do we have any idea of what Judas Iscariot expected to gain from his act of betrayal? On the face of it, thirty pieces of silver. A sizable sum, probably today equivalent to several thousand dollars. But he seems not to have thought out the consequences of his being successful, and certainly the money did him no good. There are two versions of his fate, neither of them of the "happily ever after" variety. The first, in the Acts of the Apostles, thought to have been written by Luke as a continuation of his testimony, relates that with the money he purchased a plot of land. One day he "fell forward on the ground, and burst open, so that his entrails poured out," after which the plot became known as the Akeldama, or Field of Blood. The second version, recorded by Matthew, describes him feeling so guilty over the enormity of what he had done that he returned the silver to the chief priests, then committed suicide. This left a problem for the priests, for effectively the money had become tainted as "blood money." It could no longer be returned to the coffers of the Temple, so was used to buy a plot of land which became known as the Potters Field in which foreigners were to be buried. Whichever is correct, certainly there was an area of the Hinnom Valley used for burials up until the seventeenth century.

Meanwhile, all the terrors that had so filled our victim's mind during his prayers were about to be unleashed for real. . . .

5

The First Interrogation

✛

OUR VICTIM was now firmly bound and in the custody of professional guards, his life's very last minutes of freedom at an end. While today we calculate from midnight as the start of a new day, first-century Jews calculated each day as from nightfall to nightfall. So, at whatever time of the evening Jesus was arrested, the Friday had already begun, with the Sabbath—and none other than a Passover Sabbath—due to begin with the appearance of the first star around sunset. In the interests of justice, it might therefore have been expected that Jesus would be kept in prison during the Passover festivities. As he had earlier been openly preaching in the Temple, he was hardly a dangerous terrorist. So a proper trial and sentencing could surely have waited until the festival was over. Yet, as the subsequent chain of events made clear, Jesus' captors, now that they had their quarry in their power, were insistent on moving things along in fast-track mode. They wanted him off their hands—and out of the way for good—as quickly and as secretly as possible.

Where was our victim taken? All the testimonies agree that the guards who arrested Jesus led him to the chief priests' residence for immediate, overnight interrogation. As we have already seen, this may have stood on the very same Mount Zion also occupied by the Last Supper house, where we believe Jesus ate his last meal. An alternative is a house known as the "Burnt House," where Israeli archaeologists found the remains of much fine furniture, and ritual baths as those used by priests. This and another candidate, the Palatial Mansion, were located a couple of hundred yards closer to the Temple, and inside the city walls in the southwestern sector of the city. This would therefore have involved a shorter journey. Either way, for part of the journey Jesus would have been hustled back along the very same path that he had walked in freedom with his disciples little more than a couple of hours before.

How was the interrogation conducted? According to the Matthew, Mark, and Luke testimonies, not only the High Priest Caiaphas, but the whole Sanhedrin, the Jews' equivalent of the Senate, were involved in the sometimes violent and abusive interrogation that ensued overnight that same night. And just such a full assembly of the Sanhedrin, hungry for Jesus' blood, has been portrayed in Mel Gibson's movie *Passion of the Christ*, one that has certainly not helped the anti-Semitism criticisms that the movie has received.

However, as some very sound Jewish scholars have pointed out, the Sanhedrin comprised seventy-one members. These were respected elders of the community, including Pharisees, many of them inevitably getting on in years. Though the High Priest was certainly their chairman, it was unheard of for them to meet at night, particularly at a time when there was no special emergency. It is therefore highly unlikely that Caiaphas would ever have sent messengers around Jerusalem, getting all these individuals out of their beds to question a man who had been readily accessible in the Temple throughout the previous week.

In respect to these events, whoever provided the John testimony again appears to have been better informed than the authors of the other three versions. John describes Jesus as being taken bound first to Annas, the former High Priest and father-in-law to the current High Priest, Caiaphas, then on to Caiaphas himself, both of these individuals seemingly living on the same premises. This same testimony makes absolutely no mention of any assembling of the Sanhedrin, and it is not impossible that such mentions in the Matthew, Mark, and Luke testimonies were anti-Semitic scribal additions to later manuscript copies of these gospels.

Was Jesus left on his own to face his accusers? Although most of Jesus' disciples appear to have run off when he was arrested, all four testimonies describe the fisherman Simon Peter as having been one of two disciples who boldly followed the guards who hurried Jesus to the High Priest's mansion. The John testimony is particularly interesting and authoritative on this episode because it describes the second, unnamed disciple as an individual "known to the High Priest" (John 18:15) and thereby able to gain entry inside the mansion to witness the proceedings. There is quite a possibility that he was the 'John' author himself. Whoever he was, he was sufficiently "in" with the high priestly circles so that he persuaded the guards at the door to allow Peter to come inside with him to listen to the High Priests interrogating Jesus (John 18:16). From John's ongoing description, the area where this was happening would appear to have been an open courtyard, with blazing braziers providing light and warmth, and various servants and guards standing around.

And it was just such accepted bystander status in "enemy" surroundings that would put Peter's nerve to a test in a manner that Jesus himself had all too poignantly predicted. As the John testimony relates:

> The girl on duty at the door said to Peter, "Aren't you another of that man's disciples?"

Warming himself, standing only a few yards from where Jesus was on trial for his life, Peter emphatically denied any such association. "I am not."

As the proceedings continued, Peter answered another two challenges that he was a disciple of Jesus with similarly firm denials, the final of these being at the same time that a cock crowed heralding the dawn. Consumed as Peter was by fear, for him the heart-wrenchingly uncanny aspect of this seemingly "normal" bird sound was that only hours earlier, as he and Jesus had been walking back from the house of the Last Supper, he had solemnly assured Jesus that he would never ever disown him. And Jesus had equally solemnly pronounced:

In truth I tell you, this very night, before the cock
crows, you will have disowned me three times.
(Matthew 26:34)

Is there likely to be any truth to this scene? It is this
sort of story, of Peter, the "Rock," later to be the first
Pope, portrayed in such a shameful light at the very start
of Jesus' sufferings, which speaks volumes for the four
testimonies being closely based on true happenings. People tend not to invent stories that are against themselves
unless that was really what happened. That is exactly
what we have here. And we must also infer that only Peter
himself, or that unnamed other disciple "known to the
priest," could possibly have been in a position to be able
to pass the story down to us. In the case of this part of the
John testimony, we seem to have as near eyewitness reporting as possible.

This said, the Matthew, Mark, and Luke testimonies—
which also include versions of Peter's denial—actually
provide more of what transpired between Jesus and his
two priestly accusers than does John. Although Jesus had
first been brought before veteran High Priest Annas, the
key player in the drama has to have been his son-in-law
Caiaphas. As noted earlier, Caiaphas had been holding
the High Priest office from A.D. 18, and he would therefore have been thoroughly confident of the power that he
was able to wield over this tiresome Galilean upstart who
had dared challenge the way he ran things at "his" Temple.

What do we know about this Caiaphas? Thanks to
some recent Israeli archaeological findings, there has
been a tantalizingly close opportunity to put a face to the

man. In 1990 Israeli workmen were building a new water park, just south of Old City Jerusalem, when they came across a cave containing a series of stone ossuaries, or bone boxes that, because of their high craftsmanship, can be securely dated synchronous to Herod's Temple, that is from circa 30 B.C. to A.D. 70. One of these ossuaries clearly bore in inscribed Hebrew letters the name "Yehosef bar Qayafa," that is, Joseph son of Qayafa, the Jewish rendering of Caiaphas's name. Inside the box the archaeologists who had been called in found the bones of four children and an adult woman, together with those of a man aged about sixty.

This latter skeleton was readily consistent with Caiaphas's age at the time that he died. Frustratingly, almost anywhere other than in Israel archaeologists would have been allowed to call upon the latest scientific techniques of making a facial reconstruction from the skull. We would thereby have been able to "see" the face of the man confronting Jesus in a totally real way, as distinct from the fictional representation in the Gibson *Passion* movie. But in Israel ultra-orthodox extremists insist on the immediate reburial of any ancient human remains, so no such reconstruction was possible in this instance.

In support of the argument that Caiaphas did not summon the full Sanhedrin to his house that night, it is surely pertinent that only his father-in-law Annas is named as having some additional say in the interrogation. The only other individuals playing an active, indeed, rather overactive, role were the priestly establishment's guards, whose duties standing in the background seem to have extended beyond mere protection. Anytime that Jesus made a per-

8—Physical evidence of the Jerusalem High Priest Caiaphas, whom
the testimonies name as Jesus' interrogator. A superbly crafted ossuary, or
bone box, of the first century A.D., found in 1990 in an ancient burial cave
during the construction of a water park south of Jerusalem. The ossuary's
sides are twice inscribed "Yehosef bar Qayafa" (the lettering seen in the
inset), that is, "Joseph, son of Caiaphas." The Jewish historian Josephus
independently recorded this as the full name of the Caiaphas who held the
High Priest's office in Jesus' time. It was this Caiaphas who conducted the
fateful nighttime interrogation of Jesus. Inside the ossuary, among other
bones, was the skeleton of a man who had been around sixty years old at the
time of his death.

tinent point, such as protesting how openly he had taught in the Temple and the synagogues, the guards reportedly stepped in to administer a corrective beating:

> At these [Jesus'] words one of the guards standing by gave Jesus a slap in the face, saying "Is that the way that you answer the High Priest?" (John 18:22)

The Matthew, Mark, and Luke versions all refer to the guards similarly behaving violently towards Jesus without either interrogator voicing the slightest call for restraint:

> They spat in his face and hit him with their fists; others said as they struck him, "Prophesy to us, Christ! Who hit you then?" (Matthew 26:67–68)

According to the Matthew, Mark, and Luke versions, Caiaphas ultimately put to Jesus the key question of whether he was the Jewish people's expected Messiah. Their accounts then differ on the directness or otherwise with which Jesus responded. Nonetheless, all agree that, rather than any denial, Jesus positively affirmed his Messiah status by quoting from a psalm of King David directly alluding to this:

> From this day onward you will see the Son of Man seated at the right hand of the Power [i.e., God] and coming on the clouds of heaven (Matthew 26:64)

At this declaration Caiaphas reportedly tore his priestly robe as a ritual token that Jesus had effectively signed his own death warrant. He pronounced that as Jesus had uttered an obvious, blatant blasphemy, no further witnesses were necessary. Whoever was present on the interrogation side that night, they collectively decided that Jesus deserved to die.

Was there any justification for the verdict handed down by Caiaphas? There has been a lot of argument about how he could be so emphatic about wanting the death penalty for Jesus, merely for his claiming to be the Jewish Messiah. After all, assuming that the scriptural prophecies of the Messiah were true—as every good Jew was expected to believe—someone sometime surely had to come forward who was genuinely this new leader of the Jewish people. So why not Jesus?

Why did not Caiaphas order his own security force to carry out the death sentence on Jesus, either there and then, or in the early hours of the following day? At least with regard to any offences committed within the precincts of the Jerusalem Temple, Caiaphas and his immediate circle of chief priests had sufficient authority. The Temple, as the Jewish world's holiest shrine, included certain areas where anyone who was a not full Jew—for example a male who had not been circumcised—was prohibited from entry under pain of death. There were notices in three languages positioned at key points to reinforce this ruling. Anybody who flouted it could almost certainly have been put to death on the spot, on the direct authority of the Jewish High Priesthood, without deference to the Roman authorities. After all, within two years of Jesus' crucifixion the first Christian martyr, Stephen, would be stoned to death in such circumstances, with no apparent censure from the Roman administration. Like-wise in A.D. 62 Jesus' brother James would be thrown off the Temple parapet then stoned to death on the direct orders of a High Priest.

So something was holding Caiaphas back. In the case of Jesus, his driving consideration seems to have been to have this irksome Galilean killed without any overt responsibility for this falling on him—and as quickly as possible. This was why Caiaphas did not want to wait for the summoning of the full Sanhedrin. What he and his father-in-law Annas had held in the middle of the night was not any proper trial, but rather a kangaroo court, in the staging of which they had decided that, while Jesus could not be allowed to live, any possible blame for killing him should be shifted to someone else.

Here even the most tacit admission from Jesus that he was some kind of Messiah, however unworldly, could only play into their hands. The very rite of anyone becoming the "Anointed One" (as we have seen, the literal meaning of Messiah), conferred kingship of the Jewish people upon that recipient. But kingship of the Jews was nominally held at this time by members of the Herod family, sons of Herod the Great who had been appointed by, and were totally subservient to, the Romans. So any claim that Jesus made to kingship could be construed as tantamount to rebellion against Roman rule. That was a very serious matter rightly falling under the jurisdiction of the Roman governor Pontius Pilate. And most conveniently, Pilate was right on the spot there in Jerusalem at this very time. . . .

6

The Brutality Begins

✠

OUR INVESTIGATION NOW follows the events immediately prior to the murder itself. According to the testimonies, morning had now arrived—indeed the cock had crowed, even while Jesus was still being interrogated. Whatever sleep anyone had managed to snatch overnight, Caiaphas's guards' task was now to lead Jesus to the Roman governor Pontius Pilate. As yet another indication that the John testimony was written by someone readily conversant with the Jerusalem of Jesus' time, it alone names the building to which Jesus was taken as the Praetorium. In Latin this simply means the place where the Praetor, or governor, had his residence. Since Pilate's normal, permanent residence was at Caesarea Maritima on the Mediterranean coast, we may infer that this was his temporary residence whenever he stayed in Jerusalem.

Do we know the exact location of this building? While even experts of the present day are uncertain exactly where this Jerusalem Praetorium was located, two possible candidates have been suggested. The first of these is the Antonia fortress built by King Herod the Great on high ground at the northwest corner of the Temple Mount. This Herod named after his friend Mark Anthony, famous for his "Friends, Romans, countrymen . . ." speech in Shakespeare's *Julius Caesar*. To reach it, Jesus' captors would have had to lead him through Jerusalem's streets almost the entire south-to-north length of the city, which would have meant a high danger of possible ambush or surprise attack from Jesus' supporters.

The alternative candidate, the so-called Citadel of Jerusalem, was located on some of Jerusalem's highest ground inside the gate commanding the steep western approach to the city, known as the Jaffa gate. Today partly occupied by the Museum of History of Jerusalem, from historical sources we know that King Herod the Great built a palace there, with three massive towers protecting it, Mariamne, Phasael, and Hippicus, named after his wife, brother, and friend, respectively. One of these towers still survives. For the Roman governors of Judaea, such a heavily fortified headquarters would have been strategically excellent in any circumstances of trouble, the Romans being full of such commonsense security measures to keep control of a troublesome province. This Citadel site therefore represents the likeliest location of Pilate's Praetorium.

On Jesus' guards' arrival at its entrance, the chief problem for the high-ranking Jewish priestly delegation accompanying them was that this was Roman territory that they were about to step into. To convey Caiaphas's intentions for what he wanted done with Jesus, they needed to converse directly with Pilate. And any building housing a Roman governor would almost inevitably have incorporated statues and sculptures of Roman gods and goddesses, all of which idolatrous objects would make any Jew unclean for the coming religious observance. As the John testimony specifically relates:

> They did not go into the Praetorium . . . to avoid becoming defiled and unable to eat the Passover meal. (John 18:28)

Not only does this remark reinforce the John testimony's clear insistence that Jesus and his disciples' "Last Supper" the previous evening had not been a full Passover meal, it is solely the John testimony that informs us of how this problem was overcome: "So Pilate came outside to them. . . ."

However small a detail this might seem, it accurately reflects the cultural sensibilities that prevailed between Jews and Romans at that time. It gives us good reason for continuing to regard the John testimony as including some substantially reliable eyewitness reporting. Probably the unnamed disciple "known to the High Priest," whom we suspect to have been the author of this particular testimony, followed the guard party, with or without Peter accompanying him, and he was thereby able to observe the circumstances following Jesus' handover to Roman authority.

What do we know about that authority, the Roman governor whom all four testimonies name as "Pontius Pilate"? Near-contemporary historians such as Tacitus confirm Pilate as a firmly historical "prefect" of Judaea who governed the province on behalf of the Roman emperor Tiberius between A.D. 27 and 36. The Jewish-born historian Josephus, who lived just one generation later than Jesus, recorded several instances of Pilate's ruthlessness, cracking down on any signs of rebellion amongst Jews. Furthermore, in 1961 Italian archaeologists excavating at Caesarea Maritima on the coast of Israel, where Pilate had his main headquarters, found a damaged but still legible Latin inscription bearing Pilate's name:

[CAESARIEN]S [IBUS	To the people of Caesarea
. . . TIBERIEVM	. . . Tiberieum
[PON]TIVS PILATVS	Pontius Pilate
[PRAEF]ECTVS IVDA[EA]E	Prefect of Judaea

This inscription seems to have been the dedication panel of a temple that Pilate had built at Caesarea in honor of the then Roman emperor Tiberius.

Every testimony is in full agreement that when Jesus' captors asked Pilate to provide what was in effect an "on demand" human abattoir service, he exhibited considerable prevarication and reluctance. One of his first reactions was to tell them, "Take him [Jesus] yourselves and try him by your own Law."

Why, in the light of this reluctance, was Pilate swayed? Their key argument for noncompliance, one which seems positively to have persuaded him that he had to take this priestly delegation seriously, was the allegation that Jesus was claiming to be a "king of the Jews."

All four testimonies agree that Pilate duly proceeded to question Jesus directly on this point, asking him specifically whether he assumed any such title for himself. They then mildly disagree on how he replied. According to Matthew, Mark, and Luke, he said, "It is you who say it." John, here with much fuller reporting, as from his having been present, has Jesus respond in his typical question-for-question manner: "Do you ask this of your own accord, or have others said it to you about me?" John then follows up by quoting Jesus explaining to Pilate that his kingdom was not of our earthly world, but one that was altogether more otherworldly. In other words, something along the lines of the "Kingdom of God" that John the Baptist had foretold before him.

Such an involved theological dialogue between a Roman and a Jew inevitably raises the question of how they were able to converse together. After all, Jesus was reared in provincial Galilee, where he and those around him would have spoken Aramaic, a language descendant from ancient Hebrew. He is most unlikely to have learned Pilate's native tongue, Latin. Conversely Pontius Pilate, even though he had been appointed responsible for a province where the inhabitants spoke Aramaic, may well never have bothered to learn their language.

The answer is almost certainly that Jesus and Pilate, despite their very different backgrounds, had both learned Greek as their common second language. When the Greek conqueror Alexander the Great seized the Jewish world in the fourth century B.C. he and his successors had introduced Greek as the lingua franca, or common language, among all the peoples whom they subjugated, including the Jews. And although the Romans later took over most of these Greek conquests, because of their great admiration for Greek culture, they encouraged the perpetuation of Greek as a common language in their Empire. Even in Jesus' rural Galilee, a lot of the surviving tomb inscriptions from his time, which might have been expected to be written in Aramaic, are often found to be in Greek. Likewise, when Jesus gave his disciple Simon the nickname "Peter" he was actually choosing a Greek name, Petros, and specifically because of its punning the meaning, "rock." So, although Mel Gibson broke some brave new ground by having his *Passion* actors speak in Latin and Aramaic as the languages that he supposed was used at the time, he actually missed the opportunity to get this right in respect of Jesus' encounters with Pilate. The strong likelihood is that they conversed perfectly easily together in Greek.

But if Pilate learned enough from this dialogue to perceive that Jesus posed no serious threat to law and order in Judaea, all four testimonies make clear that he was not able thereby just to have Jesus released. To add to the pressures on him to refuse the priestly delegation's demands, according to the Matthew testimony, even his wife came up to him while he was seated on the "judgment seat" to say that she had had a dream about Jesus, and that he should beware of becoming responsible for his death. So why could Pilate not follow his own instincts, and those of his wife? It therefore may well have been in some desperation that, according to the Luke testimony, Pilate sent Jesus to Herod the Great's son Herod Antipas, who like himself had come to Jerusalem for the

9—The Roman governance to which the Jews of Jesus' time were subject. [A] The Roman Emperor Tiberius, from a contemporary coin. [B] Contemporary inscription, found in 1961 at Caesarea, bearing the name of Pontius Pilate, the Rome-appointed governor named in the testimonies as interviewing Jesus. [C] First-century Roman soldier, as reconstructed from a contemporary relief. It was the 10th Legion, Fretensis (see inscription [D]), who were stationed in Judaea during this period.

Passover. Herod had recently beheaded John the Baptist, so Pilate may well have quietly hoped that he would take charge of Jesus likewise. But Pilate had no such luck. Herod interviewed Jesus, only to have the latter fail to give him any answers to his questions, so he simply sent the prisoner straight back to Pilate. Very likely he and Pilate were living within a short walk of each other inside the protection of the same Citadel/Praetorium compound.

Pilate had just one more ploy to try. According to all four testimonies, there was a custom at Passover time for him, as Roman governor, to pardon and release one prisoner in his custody. As reported in the John testimony, he asked:

> "Would you like me, then, to release to you the king of the Jews?" At this they shouted "Not this man . . . but Barabbas." Barabbas was a bandit. Pilate then had Jesus taken away and scourged. (John 18:39–19:1)

Not a single one of our four testimony authors provides any more information than the single word "scourged" for this, the first of the "official" punishments that Jesus received, as distinct from the haphazard physical abuses that Caiaphas's guards had meted out earlier. The John testimony mentions that Jesus was "taken away" for this procedure, and almost certainly it happened in a back area of the Praetorium reserved for Roman soldiery, away from the gaze of anyone who provided information for our four testimonies. Undaunted, Mel Gibson's *Pas-*

sion, on the authority of Anne-Catherine Emmerich's visions, represents Jesus' mother Mary, together with Mary Magdalen, as watching every blow that now followed. It was this gory scene of prolonged, unremitting sadism that more than any other sent shock waves of revulsion among cinema audiences right across the world, a spectacle that might conceivably have been justified had it been an authentic re-creation of how a Roman scourging actually happened. But was it authentic?

For, as with so much else in his movie, Gibson's prime "authority" for this scene was the visions of the nineteenth-century nun Anne Catherine Emmerich, as recounted to her interpreter Clemens Brentano:

> And now came forward to meet Jesus the executioners' servants with their whips, rods, and cords. . . . There were six of them. . . . There was something beastly, even devilish, in their appearance, and they were half intoxicated. . . . Two of the bloodhounds with sanguinary rage began to tear with their whips the sacred back from head to foot. . . . Our Lord quivered and writhed like a poor worm under the strokes of the criminals' rods. . . . A large jug of thick, red juice was brought to them, from which they guzzled until they became perfectly furious from intoxication. They had been at work about a quarter of an hour . . . Jesus' body was . . . entirely covered with swollen cuts. . . . The second pair of scourgers now fell upon Jesus with fresh fury. They made use of different rods, rough, as if set with thorns. . . . Under their furious

blows . . . his blood spurted around so that the arms of his tormenters were sprinkled with it. . . . The last two scourgers struck Jesus with whips consisting of small chains, or straps, fastened to an iron handle, the ends furnished with iron points, or hooks. They tore off whole pieces of skin and flesh from his ribs. . . . Only blood and wounds, only barbarously mangled flesh could be seen on the . . . body. . . . The terrible scourging . . . lasted fully three-quarters of an hour.

All this Gibson's movie most graphically dramatized, over nine to ten minutes, almost blow for blow, blood spurt for blood spurt—except, as veteran New York medical examiner Dr. Fred Zugibe has wisely commented, if Jesus really had been subjected to a scourging of this intensity and gore, "he would have died long before carrying the cross," let alone survived for the crucifixion proper.

The fact is that we do know a reasonable amount about Roman scourging from mentions of it in Roman literature, from depictions of the scourge weapon on Roman coins, and from an actual example of a scourge weapon found at Herculanaeum. All these give a far more accurate description of a scourging than the Gibson/Emmerich scenario. Rather than the rods and other instruments described by Emmerich, the actual weapon used was a *flagrum,* a whip with leather or rope thongs to which were attached pellets of metal, or sometimes bone, called *plumbatae*. These were added to inflict the maximum pain.

Intriguingly, the one "document" that illustrates the

scourging procedure with total historical fidelity is the imprint, that appears to be from a human body, on the controversial "Shroud," said to have wrapped Jesus' body after the crucifixion, preserved in Turin, Italy. Historical sources describe scourging victims to have been fully naked during the punishment, a detail which, though Gibson's film prudishly shrank from it, is readily apparent on the Shroud of Turin in the form of dumbbell-shaped marks peppering the back of the body from shoulders to ankles, and extending to the front. This convincingly shows the way that the whip, held at hand height, was lashed first in one direction and then another.

The medical examiner, Doctor Zugibe, together with a Los Angeles–based counterpart, the late Dr. Robert Bucklin, both spent decades studying the Shroud's imprint from a forensic viewpoint. Both specialists found the dumbbell-shaped marks to be absolutely consistent with contusions from lashings with a Roman *flagrum*. While the Shroud "scourge marks" are nothing like as extensive as the "entire body an open wound" scenario portrayed in Gibson's *Passion*, Zugibe has nonetheless envisaged:

> Large black-and-blue and reddish purple bruises, lacerations (tears), scratches, welts, and swellings . . . all over the front and back of the victim's body. . . . The victim's breathing would be severely affected because the severe blows to the chest would cause excruciating rib pain and splinting every time he attempted to take a breath. The intercostal muscles, located between the ribs and the back and chest muscles, would be hemorrhagic and the lungs lac-

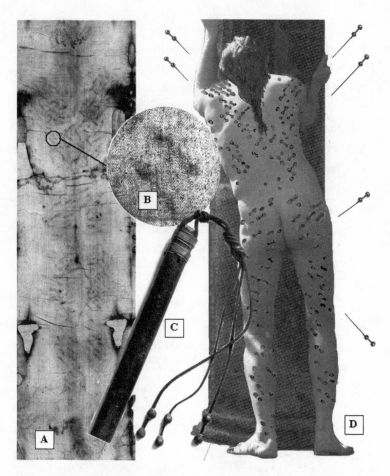

10—"Pilate then had Jesus taken away and scourged" (John 19:1). How the controversial Shroud preserved in Turin may provide unique forensic information concerning this punishment of Jesus: [A] The back of the body imprint on the Shroud, showing a full-length body covered in dumbbell-shaped marks, seen in close-up [B]. In the foreground [C] is the weapon that the Romans called the flagrum, tipped with metal pellets in the shape of dumbbells. [D] Reconstruction of the pattern of injuries as they would have appeared on the victim's actual body, mirror-reversed because the Shroud imprint is necessarily a mirror-reverse of the body that it theoretically once wrapped.

erated, badly bruised, and frequently collapsed, all of which would have contributed to the severe pain.

But in true Roman usage—as distinct from the Emmerich/Gibson imaginings—scourging, like the antics of picadors and toreadors preceding the matador at a Spanish bullfight, was but a preliminary "softening up" to the real torture that was to follow.

7

Sentenced to Death

✠

WITH OR WITHOUT the bloody excesses of the Gibson movie, Jesus' scourging must have rendered him a very sorry spectacle indeed, wracked with pain, gasping for breath, and covered with great, purplish bruise marks, many no doubt oozing blood from breaks in the skin at each point of impact. Even so, the Roman soldiers who had inflicted this punishment had not finished with him. According to the John testimony, they

> twisted some thorns into a crown and put it on his head and dressed him in a purple robe. They kept coming up to him and saying "Hail, king of the Jews!" and slapping him in the face. (John 19:2–3)

The Matthew and Mark testimonies likewise describe this same bizarre "crown of thorns" indignity, though Luke curiously omits it. The likelihood is that lying around the soldiers' quarters, where we have envisaged Jesus receiving his scourging, there were quantities of thorn branches. With wood always being a scarce commodity around Jerusalem, the soldiers had probably gathered these as fuel for the fires to keep themselves warm during the cold Jerusalem nights at this time of year, just as there had been fires in the High Priests' courtyard. No doubt some bully boy soldier hit upon the idea of twisting some of the thorn branches into a mock crown, then performing a heavy-handed "coronation" upon this unlikely looking "king of the Jews." For good measure he even threw over the prisoner's bloody shoulders an old cloak, as a "royal robe," to complete his handiwork. In all history, Jesus is the sole individual ever recorded to have received such a mockery, and if only for this reason of singularity, it carries all the hallmarks of its having been a real occurrence.

Again, the Turin Shroud's enigmatic imprint serves to provide a rather more authentic and credible glimpse of this crowning with thorns than does the Gibson movie's imaginings. On the Shroud image, all around the top of the head area there are puncture wounds from which rivulets of apparent blood have flowed as if from something spiked thrust on the head. On the body imprint's front half there are trickles on the forehead, one in the shape of a "3," as if the brow was furrowed with intense pain at the time. On the back of the head the number and distribution of the rivulets suggests something more like a crudely fastened clump of thorns rather than the neatly plaited circlet often imagined by artists. As pointed out by medical examiner Dr. Fred Zugibe, the human head area

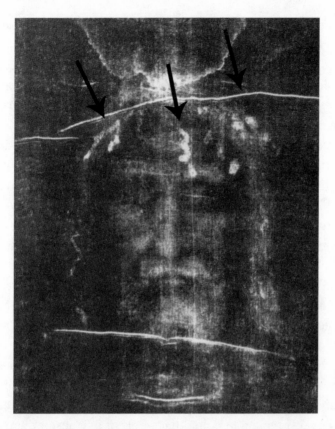

11—"They dressed him up in purple, twisted some thorns into a crown and put it on him. And they began saluting him, 'Hail, king of the Jews!'" (Mark 15:17–18). Crowning with thorns was not a normal part of the preliminaries of a Roman crucifixion, and it seems to have been uniquely inflicted upon Jesus because of the allegations that he claimed to be king of the Jews. The photograph shows the hauntingly lifelike face that is visible on the Turin Shroud when it is viewed in negative. In this form the bloodstains (arrowed) show up in white, and a convincing series of rivulets can be seen all around the forehead, also all around the back of the head area.

Forensic specialists, such as the New York medical examiner Dr. Fred Zugibe, have noted that the wounds' extensiveness suggests not the mere neat circlet often imagined by artists but a horrendously prickly clump that was thrust hard onto the scalp to cause the maximum amount of pain.

is covered with the most dense and intricate network of blood vessels and nerve endings. Any plunging of thorn spikes into these, as from the repeated blows to the face and head described in the testimonies, would have triggered severe pains resembling a red-hot poker or electric shock.

What sort of thorny plant would have been around in first-century Jerusalem to be suitable for such a crown? Lemon trees occasionally throw out from their roots long, pliable shoots bearing vicious thorns, easily twisted into a crown. The most likely plant, however, is the Syrian Christ Thorn (*zizyphus spinachristi*), a member of the Buckthorn family. This grows between nine and fifteen feet tall, and it has very strong uneven curved spikes, closely spaced and thereby consistent with what can be seen on the Turin Shroud. Another possibility is the thorny acacia (*acacia nilotica*) which is abundant in Jerusalem's surrounding hills. Amongst the many claimed relics of Jesus scattered around Europe there are odd individual thorns and the occasional crown. Of the latter, the most reputable is one that was kept in Constantinople during the first millennium A.D., then in the mid-thirteenth century was acquired by the saintly French king Louis IX. Louis built the beautiful Sainte-Chapelle in Paris to preserve this relic. But this seems to have long lost its thorns, being essentially just a branch bent into a circle, and no serious deductions can be made from it.

With the priestly delegation and the Temple guards all still insistent on their remaining outside the Praetorium, Pilate slipped inside the building to catch up on how Jesus had fared under the soldiers' scourging. Seeing Jesus clad only in an old cloak, covered with bloody pellet marks, and with great trickles of blood coursing down his forehead from the mock crown, even he, hardened Roman administrator that he was, seems to have been moved to use this sorry spectacle to try to persuade the priestly delegation that their prisoner had surely suffered enough. According to the John testimony:

> Pilate came outside again and said to them, "Look, I am going to bring him out to you to let you see that I find no case against this man." Jesus then came out wearing the crown of thorns and the purple robe. Pilate said "Here is the man." When they saw him, the chief priests and the guards shouted "Crucify him! Crucify him!" (John 19:4–6)

Pilate tried several more times to persuade the priests and the guards to relieve him of any further responsibility for executing Jesus. So, why was he not able to follow his own inclinations? The priests would have nothing of it, at this point using their trump card. As the John testimony continues, they told him:

> "If you set him [Jesus] free you are no friend of Caesar's; anyone who makes himself king is defying Caesar." Hearing these words, Pilate had Jesus brought out and seated him on the chair of judgment at a place called the Pavement, in Hebrew Gabbatha. It was the Day of Preparation, about the sixth hour. "Here is your king," said Pilate to the Jews. But they shouted, "Away with him, away with

him, crucify him." Pilate said, "Shall I crucify your king?" The chief priests answered, "We have no king except Caesar." So at that point Pilate handed him over to be crucified. . . ." (John 19:12–16)

Neither this John testimony, nor the equivalent passages in Mark's and Luke's versions, makes any mention of the famous episode of Pilate washing his hands of responsibility for shedding Jesus' blood. This particular scene only occurs in the Matthew testimony, the version that Mel Gibson dramatized in his *Passion* movie. And it is thereby again only in the Matthew testimony that there occurs the Jewish "crowd"—notably "every one of them"—reportedly responding "Let his blood be on us and on our children!" (Matthew 17:25) The terrible aspect of this passage is that repeatedly it has been used over the centuries to fuel anti-Semitism—as an indictment that "the Jews" as an entire people should be regarded as responsible for Jesus' death throughout all time. And by including this episode in his *Passion* movie Mel Gibson was only perpetuating what may well have been another of those late, anti-Semitic, and historically weak scribal additions to the Matthew testimony.

For, if the John testimony is followed as the more authoritative (and note how John conscientiously observed the day and the hour; "It was the Day of Preparation, about the sixth hour"), essentially the only people gathered outside Pilate's Praetorium shouting for Jesus' crucifixion that fateful Friday morning were those who had brought Jesus to the place, i.e. "the chief priests and the guard" (John 19:6). There may well have been a large number of these for their own collective security while escorting through the streets a prisoner with a big popular following. But there is no way that they were a representative voice of the entire Jewish people. They were hired lackeys of a clique of high-ranking priests who were acting underhandedly and illegally, even under their own Jewish law, by hustling Jesus off to Pilate without proper trial, then effectively using blackmail to make sure that the Roman administered the death penalty. It is for this reason that the now inevitable execution of Jesus can be, and should be, regarded as nothing less than cold-blooded murder, with the High Priests Caiaphas and Annas as the number-one perpetrators.

Pontius Pilate, having given in and ordered his own soldiers to prepare Jesus for immediate crucifixion, still had one final duty to perform. Throughout the Roman Empire, whenever a prisoner was marched through public streets for execution, it was Roman practice for a placard-type notice to accompany him, detailing for all to see his name and the crime that he had committed. In the case of a crucifixion, this same placard would then be affixed in a clearly visible place on the cross while the prisoner hung on it. It is again the John testimony that alone describes a little tussle between Pilate and the priestly delegation about how this should be worded:

> Pilate wrote out a notice. It ran: "Jesus the Nazarene, King of the Jews" . . . and the writing was in Hebrew, Latin, and Greek. So the Jewish chief priests said to Pilate, "You should not write 'King of the Jews,' but that the man said, 'I am King

of the Jews,'" Pilate answered, "What I have written, I have written." (John 19:19–22)

Given that the notice's first line was in the Jewish language, it is most unlikely that Pilate personally lettered
the placard that would actually be carried through the
streets. He simply dictated the wording, and then had a
scribe write out the trilingual placard.

A key piece of data for our crime scene investigation
may exist in the form of an ancient fragment of walnut
wood that is certainly purported to be the remains of this
original placard. Preserved in one of Rome's most ancient
churches, that of Santa Croce in Gerusalemme ("Holy
Cross of Jerusalem"), this came to light there in 1492, after having been overlooked for several centuries. The
Santa Croce church is so named because it houses what
is claimed to be a piece of Jesus' cross, found by Empress
Helena, mother of the first Christian Roman emperor,
Constantine the Great, when she journeyed to Jerusalem
in A.D. 327. Her purpose in making the journey was to un-
earth Jesus' tomb after it had been covered over for two
centuries by a Roman temple of Venus. And reputedly,
when she indeed found the tomb, there inside was some
wood from Jesus' cross, and also the trilingual "Jesus the
Nazarene" placard ordered by Pilate.

Originally painted white with red lettering on it, the
placard has certainly suffered considerably from the rav-
ages of time. Nevertheless, three lines of lettering are still
distinguishable, the first Hebrew, the second Greek, and
the third Latin. Despite one oddity—that the Greek and
Latin lines read from right to left, rather than from left to

12—"Pilate wrote out a notice and had it fixed to the cross. It ran: 'Jesus the Nazarene, King of the Jews' . . . and the wording was in Hebrew, Latin and Greek" (John 19:19–20). Could this twenty-five-centimeter-wide fragmented panel of wood [A], preserved in Rome's Church of Santa Croce in Jerusalem, be from the original notice of Jesus' crime as displayed on his cross (reconstruction [B])? Though the Greek [D] and Latin [E] lines are most unusually written right to left, in the manner of Hebrew, all the lettering convincingly corresponds to first-century handwriting (see insets). A notice of this kind was among the objects in Jesus' reputed tomb when this was rediscovered in Jerusalem in A.D. 326. It may well have already become fragmented at that time, for around A.D. 383 a pilgrim called Egeria described one section as still in Jerusalem, while another section had been carried to Rome by the original discoverer, Empress Helena, mother of the first Roman Emperor, Constantine the Great. This seems to have been the section preserved to this day.

right—there can be no doubt that the original inscription read "Jesus the Nazarene, King of the Jews" in all three languages.

Inevitably, such a relic, along with so many others of similarly uncertain origins, has long been thought to be too good to be true. However, from recent research by German scholar Carsten Peter Thiede, the possibility of its being authentic has been greatly strengthened. Thiede's specialty is lettering styles as these differ over the centuries, and according to him the style of the Latin and Greek letters strongly matches the fashion of the first century A.D. Thiede sees no great difficulty in the fact that the placard's order of languages (Hebrew, Greek, Latin) differs from that given in the John testimony (Hebrew, Latin, Greek). Anyone's memory might be flaky on such a detail, and a forger would actually be likely to carefully follow, rather than diverge from the John testimony's sequence.

Particularly interesting is the fact that the letters in the Greek and Latin lines run from right to left. Both in Jesus' time and to this day Jewish writing is not left to right in the way standard among our European language. Jews write from right to left. So did a Jewish scribe, after writing first in his own language (the one that most spectators of the crucifixion would have been able to read), scrawl beneath a word-for-word Greek and Latin translation in the same direction he was used to?

Whatever the answer, it would be in the company of some placard worded in this way that our victim now began the last walk of his life. . . .

8

The Victim's Last Walk

✠

WAS OUR VICTIM SUBJECTED to any further punishment prior to his crucifixion? Certainly. The mocking "King of the Jews" cloak was removed from Jesus, and his own clothes put back on him. These would inevitably have stuck to his flesh wherever this had already become caked with blood and sweat. He was then made to shoulder the large length of timber on which he would be crucified, and led by the soldiers out of the Praetorium on what would be the last walk of his life.

At Eastertime every year, a procession of Jerusalem's Christian community re-enacts this walk through the city's streets along a traditional route known as the Via Dolorosa, the Way of Sorrows. This follows fourteen "Stations of the Cross," designated by medieval Franciscans as key points of Jesus' journey—where he received his cross, where he had his first fall, where he met his mother, where a woman called Veronica wiped his face, where he suffered his second fall, where he spoke to women of Jerusalem, etc. Several of the commemorated incidents are not found in any of our four testimonies, and were derived from apocryphal stories originating much later. Even so, Roman Catholic churches often have their walls lined with scenes from these Stations, and Mel Gibson followed them faithfully in his *Passion* movie.

Crime-scene-wise the uncertainty concerning even the site of Pilate's Praetorium makes it impossible for anyone to know the accuracy of the route followed in today's annual commemoration. The fact that it starts at the site of the Antonia fortress, rather than at the Citadel, makes it unlikely. However, either of the two possible starting points would have resulted in a relatively short walk, probably no more than a third of a mile, to the execution site, which the John testimony specifically describes as "near the city" (John 19:20).

Both Jerusalem's annual Stations of the Cross procession and *Passion* portray Jesus as carrying—or attempting to carry—a complete cross for this journey. Was this physically possible? As has been pointed out by Dr. Fred Zugibe, if Jesus had already suffered anything like the excessive beating and the massive blood loss portrayed in *Passion,* there is no way that he would have been still alive, let alone in any condition to lift such a heavy burden. To be strong enough to carry the weight of a writhing adult male, a full-size cross can hardly have weighed less than 175 to 200 pounds. Even for a squad of soldiers it would have been highly impractical to have to struggle erecting and securing such an awkward object every time there was a prisoner needing to be crucified.

Particularly given a time when up to two thousand crucifixions might be performed in a single day.

And the Romans were ever a practical people. As known from the writings of Roman historians, the prescribed procedure was for the victim to carry only the *patibulum,* or crossbeam of the cross. The *stipes,* or upright—usually a beheaded tree-trunk still rooted in the ground—remained permanently in position, so that the crossbeam carried by the victim could simply be lifted up and dropped into position for each fresh execution. That the upright was a simple tree trunk also makes sense of a later statement by Jesus' disciple Simon Peter that "they killed him by hanging him on a tree" (Acts 10: 39).

Whether Jesus was somehow lashed to the crossbeam during the walk is unrecorded, though if the Turin Shroud can begin to be considered as possible testimony, this certainly shows abrasions in the shoulder region, as if from carrying the beam across the shoulders. Even a beam weighing around fifty to sixty pounds—again, the likely weight necessary—would have been struggle enough for a prisoner already seriously debilitated from psychological and physical pain, from blood loss, from breathing difficulties caused by all the blows to his chest, and from lack of sleep. The Stations of the Cross tradition has it that Jesus fell several times in the course of his journey. While not a single one of the testimonies actually mentions this, it can certainly be inferred from the Mark and Luke testimonies, and logically it seems highly probable. Both describe how the soldiers had to conscript a bystander, Simon of Cyrene, to shoulder the burden on Jesus' behalf, and to carry it behind him. Also, the Turin

Shroud image notably shows hazy but severe damage to the knees.

It is true of every murder investigation that there will always be a certain amount of misinformation, false rumors, and mistaken ideas that will muddy the data before the police find what really happened. Jesus' walk to the crucifixion site has given rise to a particularly famous tall tale, that of the "Veronica" cloth. According to the most popular of several variations, a Jerusalem woman standing in the crowd that lined the streets as Jesus toiled past was so moved with compassion that she rushed out to wipe his face with her veil. The image of his sweating, bleeding face was then miraculously imprinted on the veil. The story appears in the Stations of the Cross, and was a popular theme with medieval and Renaissance artists. Mel Gibson dramatized it as part of his *Passion* movie. There is even a relic claimed to be the true cloth of Veronica preserved in St. Peter's in Rome.

Our investigation fails to establish the veracity of this story. The problem is that the Veronica story is entirely absent from the four testimonies, and in the form just described does not appear until the Middle Ages. It seems to have arisen from a copy of the Turin Shroud face that was made in Constantinople in the tenth or eleventh century, as a gift for the Pope in Rome, thereafter becoming the cloth preserved in St. Peter's. In Latin, this copy would have been described as a *vera icon,* or "true likeness." And as memories of its origin faded, so began the confusion that this was the name of the person who had owned the cloth, bringing into being the myth of Veronica and her veil. It is a story that we can confidently dismiss

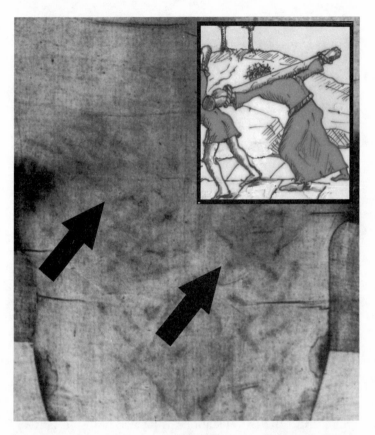

13—"Then . . . carrying his own cross he went out to the Place of the Skull or, as it is called in Hebrew, Golgotha . . ." (John 19:17). Not only would Jesus have been too weakened by the scourging to carry the huge, full cross featured in Mel Gibson's movie *Passion of the Christ,* such carrying of a complete cross is unlikely historically. Victims of Roman crucifixion normally carried just the crossbeams of their crosses, as seen in the inset, top right. The cross uprights, often the trunks of trees still rooted in the ground, remained permanently in position. Corroborating this, the Turin Shroud indicates some serious abrasions at the back of the shoulders, as indicated here by arrows.

as a fiction with no relevance at all for Jesus' true journey to our crime scene proper, Golgotha, the Place of the Skull.

So where was Golgotha? In Hebrew the word *golgothe* means skull. This translates into Latin as "Calvaria," hence the use of Calvary as an alternative name for the site. When Emperor Constantine's mother Helena made her visit to Jerusalem in A.D. 327, it was she who ordered the demolition of a temple of Venus built over the site, and who thereby found both Jesus' tomb and the Golgotha hillock on which he had been crucified. Both locations, being relatively close to each other, her son Constantine then enshrined both locations in a single, great Church of the Holy Sepulchre. Though this went through many destructions and rebuildings as Muslims and Crusaders later fought over the Holy Land, Jerusalem's present Church of the Holy Sepulchre undoubtedly occupies the sites that were first rediscovered by Empress Helena.

But did Helena, three centuries after the original events, find the true locations? Not according to British general Charles Gordon, famed for his last stand at Khartoum. Visiting Jerusalem in 1883, Gordon noted that the Church of the Holy Sepulchre—as we have seen, incorporating both the crucifixion and the tomb sites—lay within the city's ancient walls. This clearly violated the gospel information that Jesus was crucified and buried outside these walls. Wandering around Jerusalem's outskirts, Gordon found a skull-shaped hillock and an ancient rock-cut tomb that he duly pronounced to have been the true crucifixion and burial sites. These can still be visited to this day at Jerusalem's "Garden Tomb" visitor attraction.

However, what Gordon could not know at that time was that the walls that he saw and supposed to have belonged to the era of Jesus were in fact not built until a decade after Jesus' lifetime. Between the years A.D. 41 and 44, Herod Agrippa built for Jerusalem a so-called Third Wall. This was the one seen by Gordon; it enclosed the area of Jesus' crucifixion and burial. But archaeologists have since traced the line of the so-called Second Wall, and from their findings the crucifixion and burial sites enshrined in today's Church of the Holy Sepulchre quite definitely lay outside this in Jesus' time. They thereby readily conform to the John testimony's information that the place where Jesus was crucified was outside the city, but sufficiently near that many passing by were readily able to read the placard describing him as "King of the Jews" (John 19:20).

And if from these findings we can be reasonably confident that the "Golgotha" housed within today's Church of the Holy Sepulchre was the Golgotha on which Jesus was crucified, it immediately makes nonsense of another sequence in the Gibson *Passion* movie. In the movie Jesus and his cross-bearer, Simon of Cyrene, are seen struggling up a horrendously steep hill set some considerable distance outside Jerusalem. The Golgotha housed within the Church of the Holy Sepulchre was nothing of this kind. Even though to accommodate it within a church Constantine the Great's engineers and architects undoubtedly deprived us of any real feel for the original landscape, it cannot have been more than a relatively low hillock standing a few paces outside the walls. There can be little doubt that it was the regular place where crucifixions were carried out. A near-contemporary author, Quintilian, specifically described the Romans as choosing to carry out their crucifixions in well-frequented thoroughfares, so that the greatest number of people could "watch and experience the horror of it." And more crucifixions were carried out in Judaea than in any other Roman province. There can be little doubt that the hillock Golgotha, with its proximity to Jerusalem's walls, would have been chosen so that citizens could see what took place and be suitably deterred from committing the same crime as displayed on the victim's placard.

Ironically, what the Gibson movie actually failed to do, for all the excessive brutality and gore with which it represented the scourging, was actually show the crucifixion itself—*the* central point of Jesus' sufferings—in that full horror. As a punishment, crucifixion was reserved solely for Roman society's lowest of the low, slaves, traitors, and rebels, never for a Roman citizen. Roman historians viewed the punishment with such revulsion that all too few left any detailed description. Nonetheless evident from the writings of the Jewish historian Josephus is that even the threat of a crucifixion could be sufficient to subjugate a whole city. Josephus described how a particularly well-liked Jew was captured by the Romans during the Jewish revolt one generation after Jesus' death. The Romans were besieging the Jew's city, which he had slipped out of to carry out a raid on them, only to be caught. So the Romans simply set up a cross just outside the city's

walls, and showed every sign that they were about to crucify their captive. The city actually surrendered rather
than watch him be subjected to that particular form of
death.

So what exactly was it about crucifixion that was so
horrifying?

9

Cold-Blooded Murder

✠

"CRUCIFY HIM! Crucify him!" Those were the demands that the High Priest's delegation had so enthusiastically shouted to Pilate, urging their guard employees to ask for the same. Well, now they were about to get their way.

The Roman politician Cicero called crucifixion "the most cruel and terrible of punishments," one normally reserved for slaves, thieves, and rebels. At least Jesus was not to be alone enduring it. According to the John testimony "they (the Romans) crucified him with two others, one on either side, Jesus being in the middle" (John 19: 18). But quite evident from the Matthew, Mark, and Luke versions is that these two others were either terrorists or thieves, depending on which translation is preferred. Certainly they were individuals who had been properly tried, found guilty, and sentenced for crimes recognized in any society as deserving punishment. Their killing was legal capital punishment. That of Jesus was cold-blooded murder.

What was the crucifixion procedure as carried out by Romans? The first stage was for the victim to be stripped of his clothing. Given all the blood and sweat with which Jesus' body would have been caked when his clothing was returned to him after the scourging, this was all part of the torture. We all know the pain when even a small bandage is pulled sharply away from our skin. Imagine how many times worse this would have been when the "bandaging" was full-length clothing.

Was our victim clothed or naked for the crucifixion? Stripping the victim fully naked, as the Roman procedure demanded, was not only humiliating for the person, it offended Jewish sensibilities rather worse than other peoples. The Jewish scriptures forbade nudity in any public place, and none of the four testimony authors can even bring themselves to describe this removal of Jesus' clothes. This can only be inferred from their descriptions of the four-man execution squad dividing his garments between them (John 19:23). To this day, crucifixes in Christian churches almost invariably represent Jesus with a loincloth. This is partly because in the middle of the sixteenth century Pope Paul IV, reacting to the full nudities in Michelangelo's *Last Judgment* (which he ordered to be covered over), expressly forbade that anything of this kind should ever again appear in Christian art. Mel Gibson, despite all his zeal to be ultrarealistic and truthful in his *Passion* movie, likewise shrank from going to the lengths of his actor being fully naked for the crucifixion scene. But in real life history the Romans intended that any crucifixion victim should undergo the fullest humiliation. And Jesus most graphically demonstrated his preparedness for humiliation when, slavelike, he had insisted on washing his disciples' feet less than twenty-four hours earlier.

The next stage of the crucifixion procedure was the nailing of the victim to the wood of the cross. To carry the weight of an adult body that cross would have demanded some strong nails—heavy and at least six inches long. No problem for the Romans, who were proficient iron workers. At a Roman legionary base, Inchtuthil, in what is today Scotland, near to the Roman empire's farthest borders, British archaeologists found a hoard of three-quarters of a million nails dating to within two generations of Jesus' lifetime. When the Empress Helena made her discovery of Jesus' tomb, among its contents were the nails reputedly used to hang Jesus. At least two of what were reputably four nails were brought back to Rome to the same Santa Croce church that preserves the "King of the Jews" placard. One of these, of suitably convincing size and shape, was "rediscovered" with the placard in 1492, and it continues to be housed there in a typically ornate reliquary.

Of the four executioners' task of actually driving nails into Jesus' body, again the testimony writers cannot bring themselves to say anything. This atrocity can only be inferred from the fact that John, reporting Jesus' appearance to his disciples after his death, quotes the disciple Thomas speaking of "the holes that the nails made in his [Jesus] hands." (John 20:25). As a result of this, ever since the very earliest known artist's depiction of Jesus' crucifixion—created a century after crucifixion had been banned throughout the Roman Empire—there has been a widespread assumption that Jesus was nailed through the palms of the hands. Almost every church crucifix shows this. And in Gibson's *Passion* movie the actor playing Jesus was nailed likewise, it reportedly being Gibson's own hand that is seen in the close-up driving a nail into actor Jim Caviezel's palm.

But is the palm the point that the Romans would actually have chosen for holding the full weight of a perhaps 170-pound adult, male body writhing in pain throughout the crucifixion procedure? Not so, according to modern-day medical experiments. These have shown that the flesh of the hand is insufficiently strong to avoid it being torn through by the body weight and the frenetic struggling that would inevitably have accompanied this.

Not so, also, according to the remains of the only known, certain victim of a Roman crucifixion so far discovered, a Jew in his late twenties called Jehohanan, whose bone box, carved on the outside with his name, was found by Israeli archaeologists in 1968. When developers were bulldozing at Giv'at ha-Mivtar in northern Jerusalem they opened up a complete cemetery dating from around Jesus' time. Clearly identifying Jehohanan's bones as those of a crucifixion victim was a large nail, almost six and a half inches long, that had been driven straight through his ankles. And of no less interest were scratches to the bones at the wrist end of his forearms. Seemingly from the nails that had been used to suspend him, these showed that the Romans, with their long experience of crucifixions, recognized that when you nailed

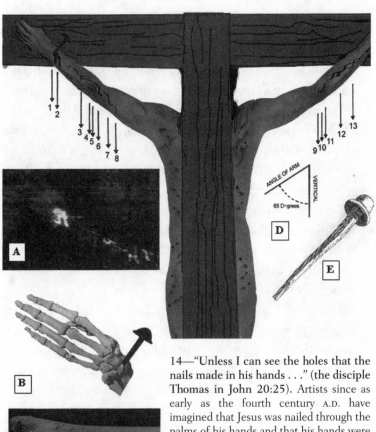

14—"Unless I can see the holes that the nails made in his hands . . ." (the disciple Thomas in John 20:25). Artists since as early as the fourth century A.D. have imagined that Jesus was nailed through the palms of his hands and that his hands were fastened to the front of the cross. However, the forearm area on the Shroud of Turin [A] clearly indicates a major blood flow issuing from a point between the bones of the wrist [B]. This is independently supported by the only known victim of crucifixion to have been archaeologically excavated, whose lower forearm bone bears a distinctive indentation [C] (arrowed) as if from the chafing of a nail. The direction of the blood flows on the Shroud, and their intact appearance, also suggests the angle the arms assumed during crucifixion [D], and that they may have been fastened to the cross from the back of the hand. The illustration [E] shows the appearance of one of the nails claimed to have been found in Jesus' tomb on its rediscovery in A.D. 326.

the arms you needed the strength of bone rather than flesh alone to support the weight of a body on the cross.

Also seeming to offer significant insights—this time specifically in respect of the crucifixion of Jesus—is the image on the Shroud of Turin. Even before the discovery of Jehohanan's remains, this had been recognized as showing its theoretical occupant to have been nailed through the wrists rather than the palms. From as early as the 1930s some highly respected international medical experts have tossed around some of the finer points of detail arising from this deduction. For instance the side of the forearms that we see on the Shroud is the back of the hand, not the palm side. Trickles of blood flowing down these forearms seem to have come from a wound at the bending fold part of the wrist. This has led Dr. Fred Zugibe to suggest that the nail could still have been driven through the palm, but obliquely, so that it exited through the wrists. In arguing for this, Zugibe seems to want to avoid rejecting history's many stigmatics who have displayed Jesus' wounds in their palms rather than their wrists. However, as stigmatics have widely diverged between themselves on many other aspects of their wounds (which often match those on their favorite crucifix), this is not a particularly serious consideration.

The one sure common deduction from all the medical and archaeological insights, one flying in the teeth of fifteen centuries of artists' tradition, is that it would have been via the wrists rather than the palms that Jesus' body would have been nailed to the cross. But did this nailing start from the palm side, as has almost universally been imagined because of the assumption that Jesus had his back to the cross? Or did the nailing start with the back-of-the-hand side of the wrist uppermost? As an Australian medical examiner, the late Dr. Victor Webster, has pointed out from his studies of the Shroud's bloodstains, the blood that we see issuing from the wound on the back side of the wrist shows no sign of any rubbing or abrading. Yet we would surely expect this if the back of the arms had been against the cross. This leads to two possible scenarios:

1. Jesus was actually made to face the cross, rather than to have his back to it. In Pozzuoli, Italy, there is an early graffito of a crucifixion which seems to support such an arrangement;
   or
2. While Jesus had his back to the cross, his arms were fastened by a nail driven through the back of his wrists into the back of the crossbeam, but with his body otherwise facing forwards. He would thereby have looked as if he was carrying the crossbeam tied across his shoulders, as he may well have looked at the start of the journey to Golgotha—except that he was now nailed to this crossbeam and hung suspended from it.

This latter possibility, an entirely new suggestion offered here for the first time, is based on a curious piece of evidence brought to light by certain threads from the Turin Shroud. These were removed in 1988 by Italian microscopist Professor Giovanni Riggi, the scientist authorized to provide the sample of Shroud linen divided between the three laboratories which carried out the carbon-dating test that same year. According to Riggi, he had obtained the then Cardinal of Turin's permission to take and use these threads for his own researches, and in the early 1990s he made some of these available to a Texas-based physician, Dr. Leoncio Garza-Valdes, to further his research into the Shroud.

One of these samples came from one of the "crown of thorns" bloodstains in the back of the head section of the Shroud imprint. And on examining this under the microscope, Garza-Valdes found a minute fragment of oak embedded in the blood glob. Obviously dependent on the Shroud being genuine, such a fragment strongly suggests that it came from Jesus' crossbeam, and that that crossbeam was of oak. It also means that the back of Jesus' head has to have been hard against this crossbeam, necessitating that he faced forward while on the cross. Though such a possibility has to remain theoretical because of the unofficial way that Garza-Valdes obtained his samples, it certainly supports the second of the two alternative crucifixion arrangements suggested above.

Given this arrangement, Jesus was very likely made to lie flat on the ground, face driven into the earth, the crossbeam roped across his shoulders, as his arms were forced into the right position and the nails were driven into each wrist. This would have given the execution squad maximum hold over him as they performed a procedure bound to cause him to convulse otherwise uncontrollably. It would also have helped muffle his equally uncontrollable screams, as his whole body seared with one of the most unbearable of all pains, sharp metal drilling into a major nerve. While medical examiners differ between each other on some minor points of detail, there is general agreement between them that the driving in of the nail would have hit the median nerve, causing, in Dr. Fred Zugibe's words,

> one of the worst pains known to man, which physicians call causalgia. Soldiers who experienced shrapnel wounds to the median nerve during World War I often went into profound shock if the pain was not promptly relieved. . . . [It] was unbearable, burning, and incessant, like a lightning bolt traversing the arm.

Twice, once for each arm, this lightning bolt would have struck and kept striking. Then the crossbeam had to be lifted up, Jesus hanging from it, and dropped into position on the permanent cross upright. The Gibson *Passion* movie, envisaging the raising of a huge, entire cross, includes a horrifying sequence of this entire cross, already carrying Jesus, being hauled up with pulleys, then something going wrong, sending cross and occupant crashing face forwards to the ground. Neither history nor our testimonies suggest anything of this kind. The Romans had to carry out too many crucifixions for anything so cumbersome. But in even our suggested arrangement, with four executioners, two either side, probably just manually lifting Jesus and his crossbeam up onto the upright, the pain on the dangling Jesus' part has to have been torture beyond belief. This is why whole Jewish cities would capitulate rather than watch one of their own be subjected to such an ordeal.

Nor did the torture end there. For, once the victim was in position, with the crossbeam secure on the upright, then his legs had to be secured, just as his arms had been. Since the eleventh century it has been popular among artists to show one of Jesus' feet set on top of the other, then the two fastened by a single nail. To facilitate this arrangement, it has sometimes been envisaged that his feet rested on a special platform that was fastened at foot height to the cross upright. The four testimonies offer absolutely no insights on this, nor do they even include any mention that there were holes in his feet.

Nonetheless, that foot nailing was a standard crucifixion procedure has been readily enough confirmed from the remains of Jehohanan, the discovery of whose bones at Giv'at ha-Mivtar was mentioned earlier. Because of ultra-orthodox Jews' insistence on the quick reburial of ancient human remains, Jehohanan's bones had to be rapidly reinterred. As a result, the anatomist who studied these, the late Dr. Nicu Haas, had to rush his work, which has given rise to many subsequent disputes over his findings and interpretations. Haas theorized that Jehohanan had been crucified with the single nail through both ankles. He reconstructed a very awkward arrangement for how Jehohanan was affixed to correspond with this. Since his death, Israeli archaeologist Joseph Zias and medical examiner Eliezer Sekeles have hypothesized that the bones transfixed by the nail came from one ankle, not two. They argue that the nail would not even have been long enough to fasten both feet. Their reconstruction is that Jehohanan's feet were first let to dangle either side of the cross upright, and then fastened to these sides

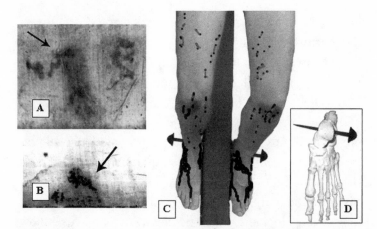

15—Was Jesus nailed through the ankles? Throughout history artists have imagined that Jesus was nailed between the tarsal bones of the foot. A common version shows him with one foot placed over the other, requiring just one nail. However, the Turin Shroud [A] shows a spillage of blood falling away from the back of the body in the ankle area. On the front of the body only part of the foot is visible, but a possible arrangement is

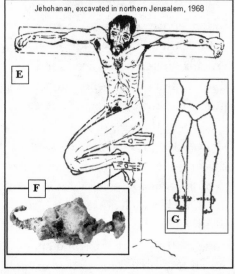

Jehohanan, excavated in northern Jerusalem, 1968

shown in [C]. Such an arrangement has been independently supported by Jehohanan [E], the only known victim of crucifixion whose remains have been excavated archaeologically. A twelve-centimeter-long nail was found through his ankle [F], and a recent reappraisal by the Israeli specialist Joe Zias has indicated a crucifixion arrangement as shown in the reconstruction [G].

by nails hammered through each ankle. And, intriguingly, the Turin Shroud similarly shows a rill of blood, seemingly from a penetrative injury inflicted at ankle height, that seemingly spilled directly onto the cloth at the time of burial.

What would have been the effect of ankle-nailing on our victim? Any nail driven through the ankles would almost surely have been as devastating on Jesus' nerves as the continuing torture that he was suffering already from his entire body weight hanging on the nerves and bones in his wrists. Hopelessly and helplessly, he and his fellow crucified could only have writhed and strained and contorted between these twin sources of unbearable agony, with death a positively longed-for release. This was what crucifixion really involved, and which Jesus—who had done nothing but heal and teach people to lead good lives—had to go through.

And in this regard the Gibson *Passion* movie, which showed the crucified's bodies relatively static hanging on the cross, could not have got it more wrong. In this so central scene to the story, Gibson actually failed to deliver anything like Golgotha's full horror, where that horror was historically and medically most justified. Assuming, of course, that a cinema audience could have borne to watch any filmed recreation of such uncompromisingly appalling human agony.

10

Cross-Check on Death

✠

DID OUR VICTIM ACTUALLY DIE? According to
the testimonies, Jesus hung enduring such atrocious suffering for several hours, the "King of the Jews" placard
mockingly displayed over his head. Passersby and even his
fellow victims jeered at him. They taunted him to prove
that he could work miracles by freeing himself from his
present predicament. Almost all his disciples, if they were
present at all, appear to have stayed back at a safe distance. Presumably they were terrified that if they ventured too close they might be snatched and forced to
undergo a similar fate. All the testimonies agree that the
several women who had accompanied him from Galilee
were present, mostly watching from a respectable distance. Described as closer at hand—indeed close enough
for some dialogue to be possible (John 19:26)—were his
mother, her sister, and Mary of Magdala, the Galilean
woman whom he had healed of a psychiatric illness. The

only male definitely by their side was the same unnamed disciple earlier referred to, in the context of the Last Supper, as the one Jesus loved. He was almost certainly the same as the disciple "known to the High Priest," present during Jesus' interrogation at Caiaphas's house, and the "John" reporting these events in the testimony of that name.

Considering that crucifixion involved no obvious, direct damage to vital organs, "only" relatively minor piercing of wrists and ankles, it can sometimes be difficult to understand how it could ever have killed anyone. In the light of the physical dynamics described in the last chapter, that question has at least been partly answered already. Nonetheless, a question that was asked back at the time of the original events, and which still gets asked today, concerns whether Jesus' death can actually have been from the effects of crucifixion? And if so, how and why he should have died so quickly? As observed from modern-day experiments, one effect that quickly shows up whenever a living volunteer is suspended crucifixion-style, even from "comfortable" straps rather than traumatic nails, is sweating every bit as excessive as the bloodshed in Gibson's *Passion* movie. New Yorker Dr. Fred Zugibe conducted one such experiment, setting up a cross in his office and monitoring all the physical symptoms suffered by his volunteers. As he has described these:

> The chest appeared fixed, and abdominal (diaphragmatic) breathing became very obvious. . . . Between six and eight minutes after the beginning

of suspension, a marked sweating became manifest in most individuals, which encompassed the entire body and in some cases actually drenched the volunteers, running off the toes to form a puddle on the floor.

Los Angeles–based artist Isabel Piczek, who sometimes needs life models to pose as if crucified for the huge murals that she paints for West Coast U.S. churches and cathedrals, has similarly noted such effects, even when the model is held solely by ropes to the arms, leaving his feet free but standing on tiptoe. Again the sweating is astonishingly copious, accompanied by chest expansion, breathing difficulties, distension of the abdomen, and shrinkage of the genitals. The ends of the fingers and toes are seen to turn first white, then blue.

Given such extensive fluid loss, and with no known compensatory intake, we might expect Jesus to have become extremely dehydrated, and this is precisely the condition that is described in the John testimony:

> He said: "I am thirsty." A jar full of sour wine stood there; so putting a sponge soaked in the wine on a hyssop stick, they held it up to his mouth. After Jesus had taken the wine he said "It is fulfilled," and bowing his head he gave up his spirit. (John 19:29–30)

One interesting aspect of this passage is that it provides virtually our only real clue concerning how high Jesus was elevated on the cross. His mouth was clearly too high for anyone standing at ground level to have been able to reach directly up to it. This means that the arms of the crossbeam were probably at least eight or nine feet above ground level.

But the other, and inevitably more crucial aspect of the same passage, is that several conspiracy theorists have suggested the sour wine to have been some kind of drug. Among the most prominent and plausible of these theorists was Hugh J. Schonfield, whose *Passover Plot* was a bestseller in 1965. As Schonfield and others have noted, Jesus' "giving up his spirit" occurred suspiciously quickly after the supposedly reviving "sour wine" has been offered him. Besides John's testimony to this effect, Matthew and Mark report it also. So, had a drug earlier been mixed into the wine as part of a prearranged "plot" to send Jesus into a deep coma, thereby making him appear dead and helping him to escape any too-prolonged suffering on the cross? Was the plan then to whisk him away as quickly as possible to a tomb where, under cover of darkness and the obligatory inertia of the Passover Sabbath, he could be secretly revived? Could some circumstance of this kind lie behind the subsequent, otherwise incredible claim that Jesus "rose from the dead"?

The problem for any such "plot," a problem that should surely have been apparent enough to anyone planning to help Jesus in such a manner, is that the Romans were far too experienced and efficient executioners to be easily duped by any such ploy. Who actually held up the vinegar-soaked sponge is unclear, Luke referring to the soldiers, the other testimonies, such as that of John, referring to "they." Certainly the soldiers were most unlikely to have drugged the vinegar, and the same is probably the case for any bystanders. As for Jesus' followers, events happened so fast in the wake of the arrest in Gethsemane, and they were so obviously terrified, that any presence of mind to prepare some kind of drugged drink—even if a formula were known to them—is highly unlikely.

What happened once Jesus had died on the cross? It is again the John testimony, alone of the four, that defines some of the religious sensibilities surrounding what would happen to the bodies of the three "criminals" being crucified this particular day:

> To avoid the bodies remaining on the cross during the Sabbath—since that Sabbath was a day of special solemnity—the Jews asked Pilate to have the legs broken and the bodies taken away. Consequently, the soldiers came and broke the legs of the first man who had been crucified with him, and then of the other . . . (John 19:31–34)

In non-Jewish Roman provinces, individuals undergoing crucifixion might simply be left hanging on the cross until they died, an ordeal that could in some instances last up to three days. But in the Jewish world any such leaving of a body on the Sabbath was regarded as an offence against God. Burials had to be performed quickly for much the same reason. And it was characteristic of the Romans to show respect towards such religious scruples amongst the variegated peoples whom they had conquered.

Their purpose in breaking the crucified's legs, therefore, would seem to have been to hasten their deaths, presumably by stopping the terrible seesawing between one source of pain and another that crucifixion was all about. Utterly exhausted, and unable any longer to gain any relief by pushing themselves up by the living wounds in their feet, the victims would simply die of the extra strains and stresses on top of ones that had already seemed unendurable. Perhaps the end came from heart failure, perhaps from asphyxiation. Medical examiners such as Fred Zugibe, who have specially researched the physiology of crucifixion, disagree between themselves on such issues because of the nonavailability of any practical way to test the Roman procedure in its full horror.

As earlier noted, the practice in Jesus' time was to count the start of each day from sundown on what to us would have been the day before. The start of the Passover Sabbath, when all work had to cease, would thereby be heralded by the appearance of the first star that evening. According to the John gospel, because the two robbers were still alive as this deadline began looming, their legs were broken to make sure that they died in due time. That this was quite a commonplace measure is strongly suggested by the skeleton of the Jehohanan crucifixion victim, whose leg bones similarly seem to have been fractured by a severe blow while he was still alive.

Did they follow this procedure with Jesus? According to the John gospel, the four Roman soldiers directly responsible for carrying out the crucifixions, when they came to Jesus, "saw that he was already dead" (John: 19:33). We need have little surprise about this. Even before he had left Gethsemane, Jesus seems to have been in a physically weakened state as a result of contemplating the terrible sufferings he was about to undergo. His lessened capacity to struggle on the cross may have been because he had suffered more preliminary mistreatment than had the two robbers or bandits crucified with him. Whatever the reason, this passage in the John testimony carries no hint of any qualifying phraseology such as that Jesus "seemed to be already dead." It is quite emphatic that he was dead. It also states that this was the opinion of the experienced four-man squad of Roman soldiers who were responsible for ensuring that everyone who was entrusted to them left them in that condition.

Even so, the Romans apparently had a fail-safe double-check, just to make sure of the total effectiveness of their procedures. As the John testimony continues:

> So, instead of breaking his legs one of the soldiers pierced his side with a lance; and immediately there came out blood and water. (John 19:34)

Our investigation has paid a lot of credence to John, the one testimony writer whom we have consistently sensed to have been a direct eyewitness of the events, at least in respect to these "last hours." He is the only one of the four testimony authors to mention piercing with the lance on the part of the Roman soldier. It can only have had one purpose, to deliver a blow that was itself lethal, just in case there could be any doubt about Jesus being truly dead. Much as today's armed police are taught to aim their guns at the chest to stop an attacker instantly (and even with today's medicine, frequently fatal consequences), so Roman military trainers taught their foot soldiers to aim their lances *sub alas,* i.e., in the chest below the armpits, for almost certainly exactly the same reason.

Clinically, the John testimony's description of blood and water spilling from Jesus' body is interesting. That any fluid should come from a dead body in which the heart is not beating has to mean that the lance was plunged into the right side of the body. Because of the direction the heart pumps, the left side of the body would have been empty. The "water" is readily explicable as from pericardial fluid that accumulated around the heart from the severe assaults on the chest sustained during the scourging. This is corroborated by the image on the Turin Shroud, which likewise shows the right side as that where the lance entered, together with a large stream of blood and watery fluid between the fifth and sixth ribs. A lance aimed from that direction would have hit the heart. So, if Jesus was not dead beforehand, there can be no doubt that he would have died very quickly from this particular injury.

We now have a dead body awaiting disposal. From all the testimonies it would appear that Jesus' body, along with those of his two companions, hung very lifeless-looking on Golgotha for some long while, awaiting someone to take charge of it to give it a decent burial. In the case of Jesus, even when that someone stepped forward, there was a delay while the necessary formalities were carried out for obtaining Pilate's permission. These formalities included Pilate sending a centurion to Golgotha to make a treble check that Jesus really was dead before

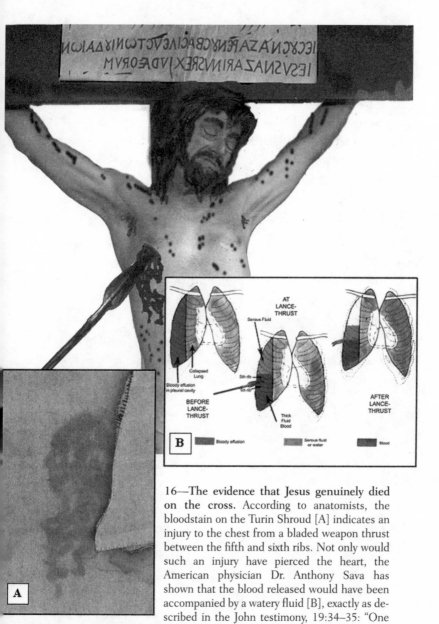

16—**The evidence that Jesus genuinely died on the cross.** According to anatomists, the bloodstain on the Turin Shroud [A] indicates an injury to the chest from a bladed weapon thrust between the fifth and sixth ribs. Not only would such an injury have pierced the heart, the American physician Dr. Anthony Sava has shown that the blood released would have been accompanied by a watery fluid [B], exactly as described in the John testimony, 19:34–35: "One of the soldiers pierced his side with a lance, and immediately there came out blood and water. This is the evidence of one who saw it—true evidence . . ."

he was prepared to release the body. Anyone who tries to argue for Jesus not having died from the crucifixion procedure therefore has to argue for the administration of some as yet unidentified coma-inducing drug, for a Roman soldier who had a very bad aim at a stationary target, and for incompetence on the part of several responsible individuals whom we would expect to have been highly experienced at diagnosing death.

Even so, there is a curiosity in the case of this particular Galilean crucified on Golgotha some time around the year A.D. 30. It is that the person whom now all four testimonies describe as stepping forward to take charge of the burial of his body was neither one of the disciples nor his mother Mary, nor his local friend Lazarus, nor anyone referred to earlier in the four testimonies. So who exactly was this mysterious newcomer funeral director? Where did he take the body? And what kind of burial did he give Jesus?

11

Getting Rid of the Body

✠

FOR WHATEVER HAPPENED to Jesus' body in the immediate aftermath of its crucifixion on Golgotha, theoretically a few brief lines of the John testimony should suffice to answer all our questions:

> Joseph of Arimathea, who was a disciple of Jesus—though a secret one because he was afraid of the Jews—asked Pilate to let him remove the body of Jesus. Pilate gave him permission, so they came and took it away. Nicodemus came as well—the same one who had first come to Jesus at nighttime—and he brought a mixture of myrrh and aloes, weighing about a hundred pounds. They took the body of Jesus and bound it in linen clothes with the spices, following the Jewish burial custom. At the place where he had been crucified there was a garden, and in this garden a new tomb in which no one had

yet been buried. Since it was the Jewish Day of Preparation, and the tomb was nearby, they laid Jesus there. (John 19:38–42)

Joseph of Arimathea, the prime mover now coming under our investigative scrutiny, is an individual who goes unmentioned anywhere previously among the testimonies. Yet suddenly we find him boldly presenting himself to Judaea's highest authority to take responsibility for Jesus' dead body. So, who was he, and what was his motive?

The John testimony says only that he was a disciple of Jesus who kept this association secret because of his fear of "the Jews." Exactly where Arimathea was is uncertain, a possible candidate being Ramathaim, which lay to Jerusalem's northwest, towards Samaria. The Matthew, Mark, and Luke testimonies are in certain respects more informative about Joseph than is John. Matthew describes him as rich, Mark as a "prominent member of the Council," i.e., the Sanhedrin. Luke, who also mentions Joseph's membership in the Council, adds that he was "good and upright" and lived "in the hope of seeing the Kingdom of God." There has been speculation that it may have been in Joseph's Jerusalem house that Jesus and his disciples ate the Last Supper, which would certainly make a lot of sense concerning the secrecy otherwise shrouding this house's ownership. Altogether more certain is that he owned the tomb in which Jesus was about to be laid, specifically described in the Matthew testimony as his own, new one, "hewn out of rock."

Only the John testimony names Nicodemus as the

man who apparently helped Joseph get Jesus' body to this tomb. From John mentioning that at some earlier time this same Nicodemus had come to Jesus at nighttime, i.e., again secretly, we know him to have been a prominent Pharisee who entered into deep theological discussion with Jesus on matters such as the Kingdom of God, and God's sending his son into the world to save mankind from its evil ways. According to John, Nicodemus procured a large quantity of myrrh and aloes for Jesus' burial. These were expensive perfumes, the myrrh probably having come via traders all the way from Arabia. Rather than for Egyptian-style embalming, as is sometimes supposed, their purpose was to counteract the bad smells which would quickly begin to come from the dead body as the decomposition process commenced. The large quantity, "about a hundred pounds," suggests that Nicodemus, like Joseph, was a man of considerable wealth.

So, within twenty-four hours of Jesus' showing his disciples the virtue of performing degrading tasks, it fell to two wealthy—and no doubt fastidious—outsiders to tend his bloody, sweaty, dirt-encrusted corpse. And, most important, to save it from being dumped into some pit for common criminals, the fate for which it would otherwise have been destined. And as the John testimony conveys, the Passover Sabbath, when they—along with all other conscientious, God-fearing Jews—had to cease all work, was already imminent. The one piece of luck on their side was that, as the John testimony specifically states, "the tomb was nearby." Even so, haste was now needed for everything that they had to do.

At the Gethsemane execution site, Jesus' naked,

bloodstained body had to be released from the nails fastening it to the cross and lowered gently to the ground. For two, most likely mature-age Jews, this in itself would have been no easy task. After all, it was a four-man team of well-drilled, fully equipped Roman soldiers who had put it up there. Once they had got it to the ground, they most likely used a simple, stretcherlike bier to carry it to the tomb. To this day such biers can often be seen still being used for funerals in Middle-Eastern countries. So, how far did Joseph and Nicodemus have to carry the body at this point?

Our investigation has already recorded that Jerusalem's Church of the Holy Sepulchre, as originally built by the first Christian emperor Constantine the Great, houses both Golgotha, where Jesus was crucified, and the claimed site of the tomb in which he was laid, both of these being within the same single church building. The Golgotha site is on the southern side of the church. The site of the tomb, enclosed beneath an uninspiring but historic shrine (often referred to as an edicule), is at the church's eastern end, a mere forty yards to Golgotha's northwest. Theoretically, therefore, the tomb that Joseph had to make available for Jesus was indeed "nearby" to where he had been crucified.

The present-day Church of the Holy Sepulchre is a most bewildering building, a rabbit warren of different chapels operated by different Christian denominations, dating from different times in Jerusalem's long history, and always under repair. Can we really believe that this was the true location where, two thousand years ago, two highly stressed but purposeful Jews carried Jesus' dead body then laid it down to prepare it for burial? The present interior edicule, or shrine, marking the purportedly exact tomb site, dates only from the nineteenth century. However, there can be no doubt that it is the successor of a whole series of earlier versions, all of which were built on this same spot. In the manner of a Russian doll, each shrine encloses whatever remained of its predecessor, all ultimately starting with the original "discovery" of Jesus' tomb itself, as made by emperor Constantine the Great's mother, Helena, back in the year A.D. 326. But so much rests on whether Empress Helena, who can have been little less than eighty at the time, really did discover the true location.

Much as in the case of the testimonies that we have about Jesus' life, the documentary evidence that we have about the original circumstances in A.D. 326 is far from as first-hand or contemporary as we would wish. The most detailed information comes from Rufinus, an Italian-born priest who lived two generations after the events. Rufinus mentioned as perhaps the best clue to Helena having correctly identified the tomb that there was found within it "the board . . . on which Pilate had placed an inscription written in Greek, Latin, and Hebrew." This is of course the trilingual placard labeling Jesus as "King of the Jews," displayed on Jesus' cross, reputedly brought back from Jerusalem to Rome by Empress Helena and preserved in Rome's Chapel of Santa Croce in Gerusalemme to this day.

And the presence of that seemingly still-extant placard within the tomb discovered by Helena has as much considerable evidential value for our own time as it does for those living at the time of its rediscovery back in the fourth century. For it makes a lot of sense that Joseph and Nicodemus would not have left Jesus' placard affixed to the cross upright, where it could only have been quickly cast away as rubbish. They would therefore have been very likely to have brought this with them to the tomb, along with his body. It was, after all, a kind of epitaph for him.

Furthermore, sufficient clues exist in and around the present Church of the Holy Sepulchre to indicate that it was founded on an area that genuinely had been used as a cemetery in Jesus' time. The excellent *Blue Guide* to Jerusalem has this to say of the Church's Syrian Chapel immediately to the east of the present-day shrine:

> Through a hole in the masonry . . . entrance can be had to a dark, rock-cut tomb typical of the first century B.C./A.D., part of which was cut away when the rock around the Tomb of Christ was removed in the fourth century. A sixteenth-century tradition located the tombs of Joseph of Arimathea and Nicodemus here. The antechamber of the original tomb may have lain to the east, and the tomb chamber may have contained ten *kokhim*, or burial places with an ossuary [bone box] in the floor. The ossuary and several *kokhim* are still visible. This tomb and a tomb on the south side . . . reinforce the evidence that the Tomb of Christ was part of a cemetery outside the walls in the first century B.C./A.D.

So, just as we have seen that the "traditional" site of Golgotha makes good historical sense, so too does the equally "traditional" site of Jesus' tomb within the Church of the Holy Sepulchre. This is the case even though all the efforts to enshrine the tomb (repeatedly ruined by equally strenuous Moslem efforts to destroy it), have made its original appearance all but unrecognizable. Which immediately raises the question: how much can modern-day archaeology still tell us of what the typical first-century, rich Jewish man's rock-cut tomb would have looked like?

As archaeological surveys have revealed, besides the rock-cut tomb already mentioned as accessible from the Syrian Chapel, there are a number of other examples to be seen in and around Jerusalem. From these, and from early Jewish writings about burials, we can determine that the typical rich man's burial was in two stages. First the body would be laid out full length on a ledge cut to seat-height within the tomb's cavelike interior. Sometimes this ledge was arched, a feature called an *arcosolium*. The tomb's entrance would be sealed up with a large rolling-stone boulder, and the body would then be left for several months or more to rot down to bare bones. Then the bones would be gathered up and put into a stone ossuary, or bone box, of the kind that we earlier noted for Caiaphas and for Jehohanan. This ossuary would then be placed in a niche cut into rock, leading off from the ledge on which the body had first been laid. In the course of time several ossuaries might be placed in a single niche, then further niches, known to Jews as *kokhim*, cut into the rock radiating out from the central "laying out" area. Apart from the two-stage burial process, the rock-cut tomb was therefore similar to the family vault that would later become popular in Christian Europe. What was special in Jesus' case, as emphasized by all our testimony writers except Mark, is that his was a new tomb, in which he was the first-ever occupant—an unusual "privilege."

Can we take our investigation any further? Despite all the long centuries of construction work over the site of Jesus' tomb, is it still possible that we might be able to reach, and learn more from at least something of the tomb's original rock surface? An Oxford scholar, Dr. Martin Biddle, has spent more than a decade investigating the site in order to find ways to save the present earthquake-damaged edicule/shrine from collapse. One of the best ways would be to take the whole structure apart, piece by piece, then put it back together again. During this process it should be possible to reveal at least something of the tomb's original fabric. At the time of writing, Biddle is waiting for the church's various governing bodies to decide on the implementation of at least some of his proposals. But the politics that surround the Church of the Holy Sepulchre—Greek Orthodox, Armenians, Roman Catholics, and others all having a say in the running of the place—make any decision-making slow and cumbersome in the extreme.

Whatever more might eventually come to light concerning this particular tomb site, the likelihood that it was the original rock-cut tomb to which Jesus' body was carried that fateful Friday is far stronger than we might ex-

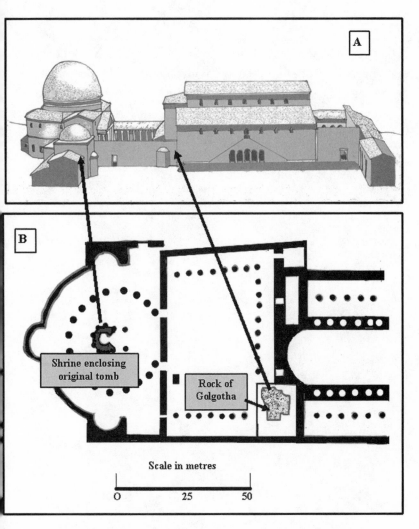

A

B

Shrine enclosing
original tomb

Rock of
Golgotha

Scale in metres

0   25   50

17—The close proximity of the reputed crucifixion and burial sites of Jesus. [A] A reconstruction of the fourth-century Church of the Holy Sepulchre, Jerusalem, as it was built by Emperor Constantine the Great following the discovery of the alleged sacred sites by his mother, Helena. [B] Ground plan of the same. Note how both the location of Jesus' crucifixion and of his tomb could be comfortably housed within the same building, as has continued through successive rebuildings of the Church to the present day.

pect. But however pressed for time Joseph and Nicodemus were, they could not lay the body, bloody and naked, onto the cold rock just as it was. Somehow or other it had to be provided with a decent, scripturally approved covering. . . .

12

Material Evidence

✠

How was our victim's body treated after death?
With typical brevity, John testified:

> They took the body of Jesus and bound it in linen
> cloths with the spices, following the Jewish burial
> custom. (John 19:40)

This obviously means that Joseph and Nicodemus
swathed Jesus' body in some kind of linen material. But
how many were these cloths, and of what shape? And
what exactly was "the Jewish burial custom" that they
were following here?

The Mark testimony describes Joseph of Arimathea as
purchasing what almost all English language translations
of the gospels call a Shroud. In the English language this
word specifically means a burial wrapping. Mark,
Matthew, and Luke then agree that Joseph wrapped Je-

sus' body in this same. But important to remember is that all four of our testimonies were written in Greek, not in the English of modern-day translations, however authoritative. In the original Greek, Matthew, Mark, and Luke's word was *sindon*, which had no specific burial wrapping meaning, and could be used of any large piece of cloth that a living person might wear as an everyday garment. Thus in the Mark testimony's account of Jesus' arrest at Gethsemane, one of those described as present at the time was a young man who had "nothing on but a *sindon*" (Mark 14:52). The arresting squad tried to grab him, only for the young man to leave his *sindon* behind in their hands and run away naked. So a *sindon* was a large linen cloth that could be used for any number of purposes. While one such purpose was as a Shroud, the word did not mean "Shroud" as such.

Throughout the John testimony the word *sindon* never appears once used in the context of Jesus' burial. Instead the word for the cloths associated with the burial preparations is *othoniois*, a plural form, seemingly signifying the usage of more than just a single large sheet. But if so, how should we see Jesus having been wrapped?

For our investigation, this causes us immediately to confront more questions. What do we know of whatever normal Jewish burial customs applied when the bodies of the rich were laid in rock-cut tombs? What sort of wrappings would their bodies have had? And what might the wrappings have been if it was a crucified criminal who was being buried?

As evident from early Jewish historical sources, the normal burial method, when a Jew died peacefully of natural causes, was for his or her body to be washed and then dressed in Sabbath-best clothes. Additionally there might be a cloth around the face to keep the jaw from dropping, and binding strips to keep the arms and legs in position. The John testimony very clearly describes this of Lazarus when Jesus called him to come out of the tomb after he had lain there "dead" for four days.

> The dead man came out, his feet and hands bound
> with strips of material, and a cloth around his face.
> (John 11:43–44)

Jesus tells the astonished onlookers "Unbind him, let him go free." Clearly Lazarus was not wrapped in any Shroud, and his bindings had only to be untied for him to be able to return to normal life. And we may infer that had he continued dead, his body, his clothes, and the bindings would all have disintegrated together during the ensuing year or so, prior to what remained being gathered up and placed in an ossuary.

But in the case of Jesus the circumstances were very different. The clothes that he had been wearing at the time of his arrest had been taken away from him when he was being prepared for crucifixion. No disciple was any-where in evidence offering Joseph and Nicodemus some spare garments that Jesus might have brought with him from Galilee. And Jesus' body was covered in blood, life blood that contemporary Jewish thought regarded as too precious to be sluiced away, and therefore had to be kept intact together with the body.

Thus, as has been pointed out by the Jewish scholar

Victor Tunkel, when a Jewish soldier died covered in wounds on a battlefield, he was neither washed, nor were his blood-stained garments removed from him. Instead the prescribed procedure was to wrap him just as he was, clothes, boots, and all, in a large, all-enveloping sheet known in the Jewish language as a *sovev*. In the case of Jesus, his bloody injuries were equivalent to ones sustained on a battlefield. All the more reason, therefore, for him to be provided with an all-enveloping *sovev* as a decent covering. Arguably, this was one and the same cloth which Matthew, Mark, and Luke referred to as a *sindon* in their testimonies.

But even with such a *sovev* or *sindon* procured, all would have been far from smooth sailing for Joseph and Nicodemus that fateful Friday. As all modern-day morticians are well aware, rigor mortis can set in quickly in the case of individuals who have died a violent death. Jesus' body would have hung some long time dead on the cross while Joseph of Arimathea hurried to Pilate's Praetorium to ask for his body. Joseph may well not have gained an immediate audience, and a centurion then had to be despatched to the execution site to report back with confirmation that Jesus was definitely dead. All of which meant that Jesus' arms very likely became rigid and locked in their crucifixion position, and would have stayed that way after he had been brought down from the cross. Definitely a problem, therefore, for anyone arranging his body for burial, and trying to get it through the narrow entrance of a rock-cut tomb.

As has been pointed out by British medical examiner the late Professor Taffy Cameron, the solution for Joseph and Nicodemus would have been to forcibly break the hold of the rigor at the body's shoulders. Jesus' arms, although stiff, could at least have then been brought together so that the hands met over the pelvis. Exactly as in the case of Lazarus, bandagelike strips of cloth would then have been used to tie them in place, and the body thereby readied for its laying in the *sovev* or Shroud.

Is there any possibility that that original *sovev* or Shroud might still be extant? That is certainly the claim posed by the very existence of the so-called Holy Shroud preserved in Turin's cathedral. And it is one not to be discounted merely because of the single, overhyped carbon-dating test carried out in 1988. Uniquely of any known ancient grave cloth, the Shroud's fourteen-foot length seems to have been chosen specifically so that the body could be laid on one half and the other half brought over the head and down to the feet in the all-enveloping manner of the Jewish *sovev*. Further illustrating its conformity to the requirements for a Jew who had died a bloody death, it bears an imprint which we have already documented, includes bloodstains as from crucifixion and from a lance-thrust in the side, stains which quite evidently no one had washed away prior to the body being laid in the cloth.

No less intriguing, and highly pertinent in the context of Joseph's and Nicodemus's activities that evening, is that some of the Shroud's bloodstains take the form of direct, postmortem blood spillages onto the cloth. On the half of the Shroud that theoretically lay beneath the back of Jesus' body, off to one side of the ankle area can be seen a stain difficult to interpret other than from blood

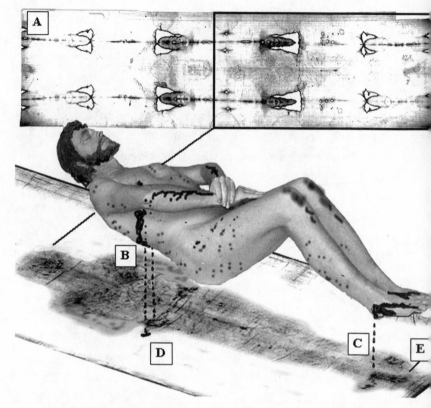

18—The apparent transfer of blood and body stains *to* the Turin Shroud (seen here in its present-day appearance [A]). A convincing feature is the way that blood from the chest wound [B], and from the nail in one ankle [C] appears to have spilled directly onto the cloth at the time that the body was laid in the Shroud. There is a trickle from one elbow that seems to have done the same (inset [D]). Disproportionate quantities of dirt have been noted at the soles of the feet [E]. Indicative that this was a body genuinely in rigor mortis is the way that the legs are sharply flexed, as if in the manner the body assumed as it hung in death on the cross. Likewise the elbows do not rest on the horizontal plane but are stiff, as if the arms have been forced from the crucifixion angle into a position suitable for burial.

that trickled directly onto the cloth from the nail wound in the ankle. Another small puddle of blood ran from a raised elbow.

By far the most dramatic of these stains is an extensive blood spillage right across the small of the back. This can only have derived from the chest wound at the front of the body, blood accumulation within which became spilled directly onto the cloth. In the case of this particular blood spillage variety of stains, it is difficult to come to any other conclusion than that they occurred during Joseph's and Nicodemus's efforts to transfer Jesus' body from the bier on which it had been transported from Golgotha directly onto the Shroud.

From a forensic standpoint, a further highly compelling element is that where the soles of the feet can be seen, the Shroud's surface, which has accumulated all sorts of microscopic debris over time, bears by far its highest proportion of dirt. When an American scientific team examined the Shroud in 1978, it was in the region of these sole imprints that their equipment produced far stronger signals for extraneous matter. This would have been from the dirt that Jesus' feet had gathered during that last walk to Golgotha through Jerusalem's streets.

Yet another highly compelling feature of the Shroud's image is its conformity to the very pose of a body that has hung dead on a cross. As can be confirmed from experiment, whenever anyone poses in the exact manner indicated on the Shroud, one of the strongest impressions is the awkward feeling to the arms. The elbows do not rest on the ground, but are raised several inches above, level with the body's upper surface. One shoulder is lower than the other. The hands rest not on the genitals but on the upper thighs. The whole feeling is of stiff arms that have been awkwardly forced into this position, exactly as Joseph and Nicodemus would have been obliged to do to break our victim's rigor mortis. Adding to this impression, the upper back and head are raised above horizontal, and the legs do not lie flat, but are bent quite acutely at the knees, both of these appearing as if they resulted from the body's last posture as it hung on the cross. Just one of many opportunities for verisimilitude that the Mel Gibson *Passion* movie had available to it and missed.

If indeed the Turin Shroud is the actual cloth that Joseph and Nicodemus wrapped Jesus' body in late in the day that fateful Friday, what did it look like? Totally without decoration, it is of pure, undyed linen, woven in a complex herringbone weave, not the plain weave typifying the fabrics used by the ancient Egyptians. This in itself indicates its procurement by individuals of wealth and taste.

In this same context a most intriguing technical feature is a seam that runs its full length, offset some three and a half inches from one edge. Thanks to recent examination of the Shroud's underside this seam has been revealed to be of a very cleverly devised "invisible" variety. Archaeologists excavating the Masada fortress on the Dead Sea, where Jewish rebels made a heroic last stand in A.D. 70, found a fabric fragment with a near identical seam. So, could both this and the Shroud have come from the very same workshop as that highly valued "garment without seam" which was removed from Jesus at the time of his crucifixion?

Following wrapping, what was left to do to our corpse?

With Jesus' Shroud-wrapped body having been carefully maneuvered onto the limestone slab inside Joseph's tomb, the next task was to pack it around with the large quantity of myrrh and aloes, aromatics that Nicodemus had already brought to alleviate the inevitable bad smells. All that then remained for Joseph and Nicodemus to do was to close off the body to the outside world using the large rolling stone boulder that stood in a special track at the tomb's doorway. Whatever the boulder at the original entrance to the tomb housed within Jerusalem's Church of the Holy Sepulchre, this has long since disappeared. However that Jesus' tomb featured such a boulder is quite evident from the Matthew, Mark, and Luke testimonies. Matthew specifically reported that Joseph "rolled a large stone across the entrance of the tomb and went away" (Matthew 27:60). And he, Mark, and Luke would all speak of this again in relation to the extraordinary developments that were about to follow.

For although Jesus' disciples had so far been mostly conspicuous by their absence, Joseph's and Nicodemus's activities had not been entirely without observers. The Luke testimony reported:

> The women who had come from Galilee with Jesus were following behind. They took note of the tomb and how the body had been laid. (Luke 23:55)

Mark noted the names of these women witnesses:

> Mary of Magdala and Mary the mother of Joset took note of where he was laid. (Mark 15:47)

Likewise Matthew:

> Now Mary of Magdala and the other Mary were there, sitting opposite the sepulchre. (Matthew 27:61)

As the testimony writer also makes clear, these women wanted to know where Jesus had been taken so that they could carry out what they regarded as their own essential funerary duties. But with the imminence of the Passover Sabbath, these duties would now have to wait until the Sabbath was over. . . .

13

On the Mortuary Slab

✠

IF THE TURIN SHROUD may be regarded, however provisionally, as a possibly authentic "witness" to the events of Golgotha, then the image that it bears can come remarkably close to our having Jesus' body in front of us on a mortuary slab. Indeed, a Los Angeles–based medical examiner, the late Dr. Robert Bucklin, actually treated it as such nearly thirty years ago in an authoritatively clinical and matter-of-fact presentation for the TV documentary *The Silent Witness*, that has never been surpassed.

To have such an "on-the-slab" facility for Jesus as he lay in death is all the more valuable because of the earlier mentioned lack of any direct documentary description of his physical appearance. This is compounded by the fact that there is no portrait of him dating from anything approaching the lifetimes of individuals who knew him personally, and who might have been able to brief an artist about his physical appearance. Extreme skepticism is needed in the case of certain claimed "portraits" preserved in Rome and elsewhere that have been attributed to St. Luke. Usually their style indicates a much later period. And as the Jewish religion expressly forbade the making of the likeness "of anything in heaven above, or on earth beneath" (Exodus 20:4), Jews quite simply had no custom for making portraits of themselves in the manner of the Romans and other contemporary peoples. So the creation of any portrait of Jesus either in his own lifetime, or for a century or more after, is extremely unlikely.

Equal skepticism is needed for a facial reconstruction that was recently made from the skull of an unknown first-century Jew, which Britain's BBC claimed as the closest that we were ever likely to get to what Jesus might have looked like. Beautifully crafted by world-class specialist Richard Neave, it is a highly lifelike rendition of the face of a Jew who may well have walked the streets of Jerusalem back in Jesus' time. But it is the equivalent of some archaeologist of A.D. 3000 presenting the face of President George W. Bush and declaring this the closest to what actor Tom Cruise might have looked like. It carries no evidential value whatsoever.

So giving the Turin Shroud very cautious and provisional benefit of the doubt, what picture does it give us of Jesus as his body lay lifeless on that tomb slab nearly two thousand years ago? The Shroud shows imprints seemingly deriving from the front and back of the body of an entirely naked adult male laid out in death, hands crossed at the pelvis. When viewed in photographic negative these imprints take on a remarkably lifelike, photographic quality still defying rational explanation. As seen on the frontal half, the face carries a moderate beard that was possibly forked, with an equally moderate moustache, possibly bare between upper chin and lower lip. Long hair falls relatively abundantly at either side of the face, seemingly from a center parting. The nose shows signs of serious damage to the septum, and there is definite swelling as from severe bruising on one cheek. This may have been sustained when Caiaphas's guards and Pilate's soldiers had their opportunities to abuse Jesus, though another alternative could be from Jesus' face having been pressed hard against the rock of Golgotha while a Roman soldier drove the nails into his wrists.

On the half of the Shroud bearing the imprint of its occupant's back, what seems to be hair is shoulder length, with what might be a further length extending ropelike down to the lower line of the shoulder blades. Not a lot is known about Jewish hair fashions in Jesus' time, specifically because of the ban on portraiture. Nevertheless, beards and long hair were certainly more common among Jews than they were among the Romans, whose general preference was for being shorthaired and clean-shaven.

Heightwise, the fact that the Shroud's exact dimensions are known, and that its images are of both sides of the body, makes it possible to try to compute its theoret-

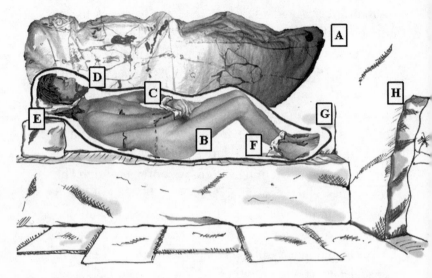

19—"They [Joseph of Arimathea and Nicodemus] took the body of Jesus, and bound it in linen cloths . . . following the Jewish burial custom" (John 19:40). The fourteen-foot-long Shroud preserved in Turin bears back- and front-of-body imprints that uncannily fit [A] when draped over a near-six-foot-tall male body laid out in a burial attitude. Attempts to reconstruct the pose [B] indicate that the head and upper back appear to have been elevated, the knees sharply bent, and the arms held stiffly over the pelvis as if there was some kind of binding [C] to prevent them returning to the position that they had assumed on the cross. Besides the all-enveloping shroud [D] there may also have been chin [E] and ankle bindings [F], which were commonly used by morticians throughout many millennia. An uncannily convincing feature is that an insufficient length of cloth has been allowed to cover the front half of the body [G], an over-generous amount having been used for the half on which the body actually rested. According to the testimonies the body was laid in a rock-cut tomb of a kind still seen in the environs of Jerusalem [H].

ical occupant's height. One method of doing this is to project and mark out on an exact cloth replica of the Shroud all the salient body features—eyes, nose, chest, hands, forearms, hands, feet, buttocks, etc.—then get volunteers to try to "fit" these in the manner of a Cinderella slipper. Just such an experiment was carried out in 1978, using cadets from the U.S. Air Force Academy at Colorado Springs. Those in charge of this experiment calculated that the Shroud man's height was probably somewhere in the region of five feet eleven inches. As this approximates the author's own height, a personally conducted repeat of their experiment broadly corroborated their findings.

Was our victim actually as tall as the occupant of the Shroud? The very suggestion of such a relatively tall height has of itself caused some to disbelieve that the Shroud, even if it genuinely once contained a dead body, could ever have had anything to do with Jesus. As their argument runs, even a century ago people were much shorter than we of the present day. People in antiquity would therefore have been shorter still, with Jesus "tall" at perhaps five foot two inches. Yet the idea that people in antiquity were all significantly shorter than in our own time is actually a fallacy. While certain populations at certain periods may exhibit some variations in height due to dietary and other factors, the general rule is that human height has gone relatively unchanged throughout the last tens of millennia. Several early English kings are known to have been six-footers. Even the first century Jerusalem cemetery where Jehohanan's remains were found included at least one six-foot individual among the skeletons that were excavated.

Physiquewise the man of the Shroud's chest area shows well-developed pectoral muscles, as from an individual who was fit and well exercised. This would be consistent with our victim's previous physically demanding occupation as a carpenter. He was neither excessively thin nor overweight. His weight has been calculated to have been around 175 pounds.

Also consistent with our investigation is that this was a man who had definitely died from the obvious injuries that he had received. There is consensus on this point among well over a dozen professional medical examiners who have studied the Shroud image. As noted earlier, it is difficult to interpret the lance wound to the chest as having been anything other than fatal. Dr. Fred Zugibe, for one, has pointed out:

> Even if the spear did not strike the heart a . . . collapse of the lung would occur because the pressure outside the chest is greater than that within the chest, causing the lung to collapse. The other lung then becomes more inflated, causing a shift of the heart structures, and . . . he would have succumbed quickly.

According to Zugibe, even if Jesus had somehow managed to survive the lance thrust, this would have been obvious to everyone around him from the continuous loud sucking sound that would have come from his body. As he related from his own medical experience:

> I responded to a call with the paramedics to a hippie commune where a man had been stabbed in the chest. . . . The man was unconscious, but the sucking sound made by air being drawn into the chest

through the blood and other fluids could be heard across the room.

Additionally there are all the earlier noted signs of the onset of rigor mortis. Among the indicators, Dr. Zugibe has identified the head and upper back raised as if from the slumping forward on the cross, the raised appearance of the chest, and a difference in density between the right and the left calves, indicative of these being stiff and rigid. Additionally British medical examiner Professor Taffy Cameron noted on the hands of the Shroud image what he called a "degloving" at the fingers, a phenomenon characteristically seen in the early stages following death. A mortician who attended a slide lecture given on the Shroud by theologian Professor Francis Filas declared from the back-of-the-body imprint that the continued tension he could see in the gluteal muscles of the buttocks was a sure sign to him that this was a body in rigor mortis.

Shroud or no Shroud then, a cloth-wrapped, still blood-dripping body—or something along these lines—would have been what Joseph of Arimathea and Nicodemus left inside Joseph's tomb, just a stone's throw from the Golgotha execution site, as dusk fell on that fateful Friday evening. To all appearances there lay dead on that stone slab a bearded male Jew who even before his undergoing crucifixion had been too weak to carry his cross the full distance to his execution site. An individual who had been brutally beaten by Temple guards, savagely scourged, and subjected to the torture of the ancient world's most bar-

baric form of capital punishment, crucifixion. An individual who even when he had appeared long dead from all these ordeals had then been stabbed deep into his chest by a professional soldier whose very job—the Romans titled him *exactor mortis,* or exactor of death—rested on those submitted to him being dead when they left his charge.

This was the body that Joseph of Arimathea and Nicodemus had secured from any outside interference by their rolling across the tomb entrance a huge boulder (Mark 16:4). Despite this boulder's size, moving it would not have been overly difficult for this pair, even working entirely on their own. As known from tombs of Jesus' time in Jerusalem's immediate environs, the channel cut for the rock's path across the tomb's entrance was typically sloped downward. While the tomb was needed to remain open, a simple stopper stone in the channel served to check the boulder from moving. Upon this stone being removed, the boulder rolled effortlessly downward across the entrance. All the difficulty—one demanding the efforts of several strong men—lay with opening it up again.

During the next thirty-six hours theoretically no one— and certainly not any Jew—would have dared to attempt anything so strenuous. This was because of the day being a Passover Sabbath. Even on a normal Sabbath the Jewish scriptures were absolutely emphatic:

> You shall do no work on that day, neither you nor your son nor your daughter nor your servants, men or women, nor your animals nor the alien living with you. (Exodus 20:10)

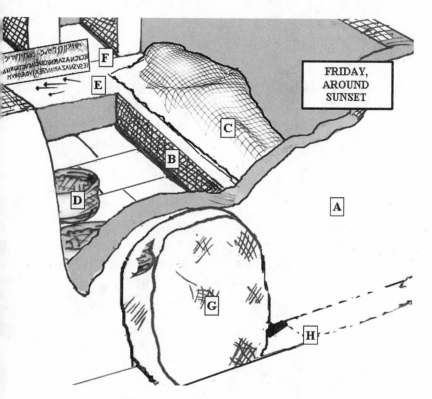

20—"Joseph...rolled a stone against the entrance to the tomb" (Mark 15:46). A reconstruction of Jesus' tomb as Joseph of Arimathea and Nicodemus left it on the evening of the Friday of the crucifixion. The tomb was reportedly a new one "in which no one had yet been buried" (John 19:41), located "at the place where he [Jesus] had been crucified" (John 19:41) and "hewn out of the rock" [A] (Matthew 27:60). Mark 16:5 describes the tomb's interior as featuring a ledge on the right-hand side [B], for the laying out of the body. The Matthew, Mark, and Luke testimonies all describe Joseph as having procured a shroud (*sindon* in the original Greek) [C] to wrap Jesus' body. According to John 19:39, accompanying this was "a mixture of myrrh and aloes, weighing about a hundred pounds." Such spices may have been stored in bags or baskets [D]. According to later sources the nails of crucifixion and the notice of Jesus' crime [E] were retrieved, and therefore these may also have been among the tomb's contents. Behind these items can be seen two recesses [F], intended for the ossuaries, or bone boxes, in which the deceased's bones would eventually be gathered. Joseph and Nicodemus' final task was to roll a large stone [G] across the tomb's entrance (Mark 15:46). Though often very large, such stones could be moved relatively easily into position with the aid of a specially inclined track [H].

Yet, as events were about to prove, someone or something within that next thirty-six hours would manage to roll that boulder back upward to reopen the tomb's entrance. And by whatever means, somehow that "dead" body would be found to have vanished into thin air.

14

Grave Disturbance

✠

OUR INVESTIGATION HAS NOTED that not a single male disciple is recorded to have been around to attend to Jesus' body—even to see how it would be looked after, or where it would be put. But the band of women who had accompanied Jesus from Galilee were apparently of sterner stuff. Of these women, who just like the disciples, had apparently also traveled around the country with Jesus during his preachings and healings, the Luke author earlier testified:

> [As] he made his way through towns and villages preaching . . . with him . . . went . . . certain women who had been cured of evil spirits and ailments. Mary, surnamed the Magdalene, from whom seven demons had gone out; Joanna, the wife of Herod's steward Chuza. Susanna, and several others who

provided for them out of their own resources. (Luke 8:1–3)

According to the Mark testimony, it had been this Mary, from the Galilean village of Magdala, together with Mary the mother of Joset (possibly a blood relative of Jesus), and a number of other women, who had watched "from a distance" as Jesus was being crucified (Mark 15:40). They had also watched Joseph of Arimathea and Nicodemus as they struggled to maneuver his dead body into the tomb (Mark 15:47).

Why would they choose to keep Jesus' body under such close observation? Because they wanted to make sure they knew where it was being taken so that they could attend to it in their own special way after the Passover Sabbath. According to the testimony from Mark, they had been preparing aromatics of their own, and with these they wanted to carry out their own funerary rites on Jesus' body, obviously before the smell of death became too extreme.

Now, at first light there were what would seem to have been at least three women hurrying through the gloom to perform this task. According to Mark the group was comprised of Mary of Magdala, Mary the mother of James, and Salome. In Luke's version the one difference was that Joanna—the wife of King Herod's steward—replaced Salome. Matthew mentioned only the two Marys. And John, maverick to the last, recorded only the presence of Mary of Magdala—except that, when he quoted her reporting her experience to two male disciples, he had her using the plural "we" (John 20:2), indicating that she had at least one companion.

At this point in our investigation, trying to establish some firm facts is very similar to trying to work out what happened at a major traffic accident from the testimony of four different witnesses, each of whom can only describe how a series of confusing, perplexing, fast-moving events looked from their particular viewpoint. Adding to the difficulty is that we simply cannot be sure which of these witnesses may have been describing the events from a much more garbled, secondhand or thirdhand viewpoint than the others.

Even so, certain commonly agreed-upon details can be gleaned. First, it was very early in the day. John speaks of: "very early, and still dark" (John 20:1); Mark of "very early in the morning . . . when the sun had risen" (Mark 16:2). Despite such differences in the statements, both concur that the time of day was around very first light, immediately after the "enforced inertia" of the Passover Sabbath.

Second, the first of Jesus' party to arrive on the scene were not Jesus' male followers, but a group of his women followers. The fact of these having set out very early with no male accompaniment is reinforced by the very question that the Mark testimony recorded the women as discussing between themselves along the way: "Who will roll away the stone for us from the entrance to the tomb?" (Mark 16:3). Given that Mark named three women as being present on that early morning mission, this reaffirms that the task of rolling away this boulder to reopen the tomb was one beyond their combined strengths.

Third, when the first women arrived at the tomb this very same boulder had somehow already been rolled away from the entrance. And fourth, with the tomb interior thereby accessible, it was the women who quickly determined that Jesus' body had most mysteriously disappeared from inside. According to Luke: "On entering [the tomb] they could not find the body of the Lord Jesus." According to John, Mary of Magdala, having established this, ran back to tell Jesus' male disciples: "They have taken the Lord out of the tomb and we don't know where they have put him" (John 20:2).

All of which might seem relatively straightforward, were it not for the Matthew testimony and some major discrepancies in this concerning point four. Of the events earlier associated with the crucifixion, Matthew, alone of the four testimony writers, described Jesus' death as accompanied by an earthquake, damage at the Temple, and dead people rising from their graves, extraordinary incidents that Mel Gibson duly dramatized in his *Passion* movie. All of these events would have been so newsworthy in their own right that if they really had happened we would have expected to hear of it from other historical sources. And we would of course have expected the other three testimony-writers to have spoken of them likewise.

Thus, when we find the Matthew testimony recording, again uniquely, the chief priests posting a guard over Jesus' tomb throughout the Passover Sabbath—then describing at the moment of the women's arrival a second earthquake bursting the tomb open and sending the guards scattering in disarray—it is more than a little difficult to take this version seriously.

Conversely, it is once again the John testimony that at this very point in the story provides more detail as from reliable, close-hand reporting. This describes Simon Peter and the very same disciple "known to the High Priest" through whose intermediary he had gained admission to Caiaphas's house, acting on Mary of Magdala's breathless alert about the tomb's emptiness by literally running to this to find out whatever they could:

> So Peter set out with the other disciple ["the one whom Jesus loved" (John 20:2)] to go to the tomb. They ran together, but the other disciple, running faster than Peter, reached the tomb first; he bent down and saw the linen clothes lying on the ground but did not go in. Simon Peter, following him, also came up, went into the tomb, saw the linen cloths lying on the ground and also the cloth that had been over his head; this was not with the linen cloths but rolled up in a place by itself. Then the other disciple who had reached the tomb first also went in; he saw and he believed. Till this moment they had not understood the scripture, that he must rise from the dead. (John 20:3–9)

For our investigative purposes, there is so much in those few words that is meaningful, yet there is also so much that remains tantalizingly elusive. Why, for instance, did this same "other disciple"—earlier described as known to the High Priest, and who was very likely the "John" writer himself—first outrun Peter, only to pause waiting for him to catch up? Why did he not immediately go all the way into the tomb? Could he have been some-one belonging to the Jewish priestly hierarchy—in which case he would have feared being defiled by the presence of a dead body. So, did he perhaps wait because he wanted Peter's assurance that, with the stone rolled back, there was no longer any dead body in the tomb before he could feel comfortable about going in? The stature of John as a witness becomes ever more advanced by such considerations.

And whatever the answer, there has to have been something quite extraordinary about the scene that Peter and "John" witnessed inside—and in particular the pres-ence and the arrangement of those "linen cloths"—which convinced them then and there that Jesus *had* to have risen from the dead. Frustratingly, and among the many uncertainties surrounding the cloth we know today as the Turin Shroud, "John," even at this key juncture, failed to make any mention of a *sindon* among the definitely plural "cloths" that he and Peter found in the tomb that Sunday morning. In the original Greek, he used the word *soudar-ion* for the cloth that had been over Jesus' head and which was now "rolled up in a place by itself." Many modern translators interpret this as just a face cloth, in which case the large *sindon* that Matthew, Mark, and Luke re-ferred to most puzzlingly goes unmentioned. As *soudarion* simply means sweat cloth, could "John" have had in mind a sweat cloth of the whole body? This would certainly be readily reconcilable both with the Turin Shroud and the *sindon* spoken of by the other the testimony writers.

Where had the body gone? All four testimonies agree that Jesus' burial wrappings had been removed from his

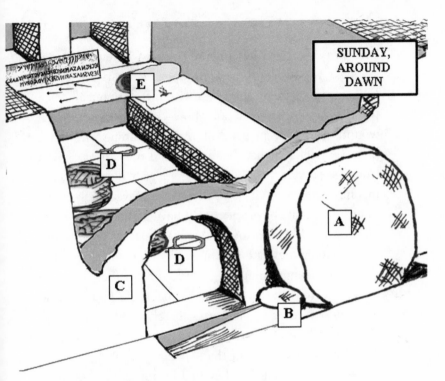

21—"Mary of Magdala . . . saw that the stone had been moved away from the tomb" (John 20:1). A reconstruction of Jesus' tomb as found early on Sunday morning. The first on the scene were up to three women, among them Mary of Magdala. They had been anticipating difficulty rolling the stone back from the entranceway (Mark 16:3), but found that persons unknown had already performed this task [A] sometime prior to their arrival. To hold the stone back would have required the lodging of a smaller stone in its path [B]. On entering the tomb the women found the body of Jesus to have inexplicably disappeared (Luke 24:3). According to the testimony of John, it was necessary to bend down to see inside (John 20:5). This strongly suggests the entranceway to have been low [C]. John describes *othonia* (very possibly the chin, wrist, and ankle bindings shown on page 140), lying on the floor [D] and visible from outside the tomb. Peter entered first, quickly followed by "John," and they saw "the cloth [*soudarion*] that had been over his head" lying "not with the *othonia*, but rolled up in a place by itself" (John 20:7). This strongly suggests John to have been describing a large cloth, arguably the same *sindon*, or shroud, referred to in the Matthew, Mark, and Luke testimonies, and presumably in situ on the ledge on which Jesus' body had been laid [E].

body and had been left behind during whatever circumstances. Yet his body had disappeared from the tomb. Raising the question: had he revived, freed himself from these wrappings, then somehow—despite those open wounds seriously in need of major stitching—moved a huge boulder that had been designed only to be moved from the outside, not the inside? Not only does this seem inconceivable, even if he could have achieved such an extraordinary feat, surely he would have gathered the wrappings around him garment style, rather than venture out stark naked a mere stone's throw from Jerusalem's walls?

What if some unknown intruder or intruders came to the tomb from the outside, rolled back the boulder, and then, under cover of darkness, snatched his body away? Again, surely any such person or persons would have kept his body wrapped, rather than specially unwrapping it to transport it to wherever they had in mind? Furthermore, the impression that is conveyed by the gospel descriptions concerning the linen clothes is of neatness and good order, as if by whatever process the body had disappeared, its wrappings had been left largely undisturbed from how Joseph and Nicodemus had put them into place. Such a sight, of the body seeming to have passed through its wrapping, would indeed have been one to cause Peter and "John" actually to "believe" at this particular point that Jesus had "risen from the dead," just as he predicted he would.

But the extraordinary happenings of that Passover Sunday morning were far from over. According to the Mark testimony, the two Marys and Salome, even before Mary of Magdala had rushed back to alert Peter and

"John," had found the tomb empty of Jesus' body, though not without an occupant. That individual's presence they only became aware of when they ventured inside:

> On entering the tomb they saw a young man in a white robe seated on the right-hand side, and they were struck with amazement. But he said to them, "There is no need to be so amazed. You are looking for Jesus of Nazareth, who was crucified. He has risen. He is not here. See, here is the place where they laid him." (Mark 16:5–6)

Luke's testimony was very similar, except that he noted that the women initially

> could not find the body of the Lord Jesus. [Then] as they stood there puzzled about this, two men in brilliant clothes suddenly appeared at their side. Terrified, the women bowed their heads to the ground. But the two said to them: "Why look among the dead for someone who is alive? He is not here. He has risen." (Luke 24:3–6)

At which point, however objective and CSI-like we have tried to be throughout the investigation thus far, consideration of some form of supernatural involvement now becomes increasingly difficult to avoid. First, every testimony describes the presence of one or more mysterious "men in white" at the tomb. Though gospel translations often use the word "angel" for these mystery intruders, it's important to realize that just as the word *sindon* meant "cloth" rather than specifically a "shroud," so "angel," in Greek *angelos*, meant "messenger," rather than specifically one of the sent-from-heaven variety.

Of all the four accounts of these mystery occupants of the tomb, it is John's that carries some additional detail that makes his testimony so particularly compelling. According to John, Mary of Magdala, after having run to alert Peter and "John" of what she and her companions had come across, accompanied this pair back to the tomb. Indeed, she almost certainly needed to lead them to it, as it was the women, not the men, who would have known where to find it. (For while the Matthew, Mark, and Luke gospels all emphatically mention Mary of Magdala and her female companions taking a careful note of where Jesus was buried [Matthew 27:61; Mark 15:47; Luke 23:55], nothing of the same kind is recorded of the men.) Then, while Peter and "John," having gone inside, marveled at the arrangement of the linen wrappings, but found the tomb otherwise empty, then went off "back home" again, Mary lingered on alone outside, filled with tears.

> Then, as she wept, she stooped to look inside. (John 20:11)

This particular piece of information from John's testimony immediately clarifies why "other disciple" John had not immediately seen the full arrangement of the burial wrappings while hesitating at the tomb's entrance. Even for a woman, the entrance was apparently sufficiently low that it required some stooping to be able to see inside, particularly necessary to view any person or object sitting or resting on the seat-height tomb ledge. For according to John, despite no one having been seen to enter or leave the tomb since Peter and his departure, Mary now saw within:

> Two messengers in white . . . sitting where the body of Jesus had been, one at the head, the other at the feet. They said, "Woman, why are you weeping?" "They have taken my Lord away," she replied, "and I don't know where they have put him." (John 20:11–13)

There is an obvious discrepancy here with the Matthew, Mark, and Luke accounts. All three of these described the women, including Mary of Magdala, as seeing one or more of such messengers when they had *first* looked into the tomb. But that is not what John conveys. However, what happened next is attested to in some form in every version except Luke's, and it is nothing less than mind-blowing. John's version, though not without its perplexities, is by far the fullest. As Mary—evidently still crouched outside the tomb while she was in conversation with its two occupants seated on the tomb slab within— "turned round" she

> *saw Jesus standing there,* though she did not realize it was Jesus. Jesus said to her, "Woman, why are you weeping? Who are you looking for?" Supposing him to be the gardener, she said, "Sir, if you have taken him away, tell me where you have put him, and I

will go and remove him." Jesus said "Mary!" She turned round then and said to him in Hebrew "Rabbuni," which means "Master." (John 20:14–16)

Can we reconstruct what was quite obviously one of the most extraordinary encounters in all human history? Mel Gibson's *Passion* movie did not include this scene because he followed the Matthew version. And if at first its impact might seem dulled because of Mary's failure immediately to recognize Jesus, this in actuality becomes readily explicable. The key lies in the *double* mention of Mary turning around, first in verse 14, and again in verse 16. This only makes sense when we properly picture her crouched at the low tomb entrance talking to the astonishing individuals who were seated on the ledge inside on which Jesus' body had been laid before its disappearance. First, while she was still preoccupied with these two individuals, she turned only half around on her becoming aware of someone standing beside her. Hence when she was speaking to this newcomer she may well have been still half turned away from him, thereby without ever properly looking up to see who he was.

Then suddenly she heard him address her by name: "Mary!" At this point the effect was electric. She immediately turned fully to encounter the unbelievable. This man whose horribly tortured body she had seen in stark-staringly obvious death just thirty-six hours before was now standing before her large as life. Just as he had predicted he would, Jesus of Nazareth had risen from the dead.

If this had been all that anyone experienced, it would of course have been dismissed out of hand as just the unsubstantiated testimony of one lone woman with an already well-established history of mental disturbance. Our investigation would have been equally unbelievable on this point. But now some other, even more astonishing sightings were in store. . . .

15

Strange Sightings

✠

WERE THERE ANY OTHER SIGHTINGS to add credence to the strange story told by Mary of Magdala? According to the John testimony, Mary, after Jesus had
appeared to her, "went and told the disciples that she had
seen the Lord," i.e., Jesus. She also reported the words
that he had spoken to her:

> Do not cling to me, because I have not yet as-
> cended to the Father [i.e. God]. But go to the broth-
> ers, and tell them: I am ascending to my Father.
> (John 20:18)

John omitted to mention the "brothers'" reaction to
Mary's story. But Mark, after briefly reiterating the story
of Jesus' appearance to Mary, went on:

> She then went to those who had been his compan-
> ions, and who were mourning and in tears, and told

them. But they did not believe her when they heard her say that he was alive and that she had seen him. (Mark 16:10–11)

Meanwhile, the Luke testimony had a fresh "sighting" to report. At a point that can only have been shortly before Mary of Magdala had returned with her story of directly encountering Jesus, one of Jesus' followers named Cleopas, together with an unnamed companion, had set off from Jerusalem to walk the seven-mile journey to a village called Emmaus. As this pair walked in dejection and despair, an apparent stranger started walking alongside them, quickly asking them what it was that made them so unhappy. As Luke took up the story:

Cleopas answered him: "You must be the only person staying in Jerusalem who does not know the things that have been happening there these last few days. He [the stranger] asked "What things?" They answered: "All about Jesus of Nazareth, who showed himself a prophet powerful in action and speech before God and the whole people, and how our chief priests and our leaders handed him over to be sentenced to death, and had him crucified. Our own hope had been that he would be the one to set Israel free. And this is not all. Two whole days have now gone by since it all happened, and some women from our group have astounded us. They went to the tomb in the morning, and when they could not find the body, they came back to tell us they had seen a vision of angels/messengers who declared he was alive. Some of our friends went to the tomb and found everything exactly as the women had reported, but of him they saw nothing. (Luke 24:18–24)

The great value of this reporting of Cleopas' words is that in just a few simple sentences it essentially summarized and corroborated everything that we have so far inferred throughout our crime scene investigation. That is: that it was Jerusalem's chief priests and leaders, not any assembly of the entire Jewish people, who had instigated Jesus' execution by crucifixion. That it was the populace's and indeed Cleopas and his companion's own expectation of Jesus that he was the prophesied Messiah/Christ who would release them from Roman domination. That it was a group of women who had been the first to arrive at Jesus' tomb and discover his body gone, encountering there instead mystery messengers who told them that he was alive again. And that Peter and (probably) John had indeed then gone to the tomb to find everything as the women had reported. All that Cleopas and his companion had not heard of up to that point—presumably because they had left Jerusalem just a little too early—was anything of Mary of Magdala's encounter with that very much alive Jesus himself.

And obvious though it should have been to Cleopas and to his companion, what they were also failing to be aware of at that particular moment was that they were already in the midst of a very similar experience to that of Mary of Magdala. For this was no ordinary stranger who had taken up to walking beside them. He suddenly began talking to them in a way that, as they later described it, "burned in their hearts":

> You foolish men! So slow to believe all that the prophets have said. Was it not necessary that the Christ/Messiah should *suffer* before entering into his glory? (Luke 24:25–26)

As the Luke testimony continued its narrative,

> Then, starting with Moses and going through all the prophets, he [the stranger] explained to them the passages throughout the scriptures that were about himself. When they drew near to the village . . . they pressed him to stay with them. . . . Now, while he was with them at table, he took the bread and said the blessing; then he broke it and handed it to them. And their eyes were opened and they recognized him. But he had vanished from their sight. (Luke 24:27–31)

The investigative mind inevitably floods with questions, many of these no doubt as unanswerable in the minds of the pair who actually underwent the experience as they can ever be in our own minds, two thousand years later. For if this unrecognized stranger was really Jesus, presumably he must have looked quite "normal" to Cleopas and to his companion as he walked along the road with them, then sat down with them for a meal. So, how was he dressed? Why did they not recognize him? What was it that made them recognize him only when they did, when he broke the loaf of bread that they were about to eat? Was it perhaps their first clear sight of his hands, and their suddenly finding themselves looking at nail holes in these? Also, just what sort of "resurrection" was this on Jesus' part, that he could walk, talk, handle bread, and appear totally solid one moment, then vanish into thin air the next?

Whatever the answers to those questions, the experience so astounded Cleopas and his companion that, as Luke goes on . . .

> They set out *that instant* and returned to Jerusalem. There they found the Eleven [i.e., the twelve disciples minus Judas] assembled together with their companions, who said to them, "The Lord has indeed risen and has appeared to Simon." (Luke 24:33–34)

So, sometime earlier that same day, though inevitably sometime after Simon Peter and "John" had left the tomb, Jesus had made an additional "live" appearance to Simon Peter. Presumably it was one of much the same variety as that to Mary of Magdala, though it has gone otherwise unrecorded, except for a glancing, later mention in a letter of St. Paul (1 Corinthians 15:5). Paul, who believed women needed to be kept in their place, notably omitted to take any account of Mary of Magdala's story, just as in Luke's version. But having been duly told of this particular sighting of Jesus, Cleopas and his companion now related their experience:

They told their story of what had happened on the road and how they had recognized him at the breaking of bread. (Luke 24:35)

Further corroborative evidence for our investigation was about to be added by other events of that extraordinary Sunday. For, any doubts still nurtured by those disciples who had not yet had any such direct experiences of an alive-and-well Jesus were about to be allayed that very same evening. As the Luke testimony continues:

They were still talking about all this when he [Jesus] himself stood among them and said to them, "Peace be with you!" In a state of alarm and fright, they thought they were seeing a ghost. But he said "Why are you so agitated, and why are these doubts stirring in your hearts? See my hands and my feet that it is I myself. Touch me and see for yourselves. A ghost has no flesh and bones as you can see I have." And as he said this he showed them his hands and his feet. Their joy was so great that they still could not believe it, as they were dumbfounded. So he said to them, "Have you anything here to eat? And they offered him a piece of grilled fish which he took and ate before their eyes." (Luke 24:36–43)

The John testimony not only describes, and accordingly corroborates, exactly this same incident, it adds to the general bewilderment. For it states that the doors to the room in which the disciples were gathered "were closed . . . for fear of the Jews" (John 20:19). Indicating thereby that Jesus' body had mysteriously passed through these doors. It also mentions that Jesus showed the assembly his side as well as his hands and feet, a description that seems to indicate his flesh-and-bones body still bore the visible penetrations caused by the crucifixion nails and the lance.

Additionally and uniquely, John told of a later, second appearance by Jesus to this collective assembly of the disciples. At this second sighting the disciple Thomas was present. Thomas had been absent on the previous Sunday, and had been expressing his disbelief of what the others had told him:

> "Unless I can see the holes that the nails made in his hands and can put my finger into the holes they made, and unless I can put my hand into his side, I refused to believe." (John 24:25)

Now, eight days after the first incident, the doors of the room in which the disciples were gathered were again closed, when Jesus

> came in and stood among them. "Peace be with you," he said. Then he spoke to Thomas "Put your finger here. Look, here are my hands. Give me your hand. Put it into my side. Do not be unbelieving any more, but believe." Thomas replied, "My Lord and my God!" (John 24:26–28)

In any normal, rational terms, all these testimonies are obviously extraordinary and extremely difficult to believe. Quite definitely not the usual stuff of any crime scene investigation. Yet, what is impressive about them is the very calm, matter-of-fact way everything is recounted, and the ready acknowledgment that even those undergoing the experiences were as disbelieving of their own senses as we can very legitimately be from our reading and listening to their story.

For, how could anyone, either in Jesus' time or now, comprehend how a man who had been so publicly and so cruelly put to death have become so *palpably* alive again? Self-evidently this "resurrected" Jesus was not a man still weak and full of pain, as we could only expect if he had somehow been physically resuscitated from that tortured, bloody death forty-eight hours earlier. Rather, he was an individual who was obviously taking some care to demonstrate that he was not in any way impaired by the ordeal. Also, that he could seem physically solid and even be eating food one moment, then ghost-like pass through closed doors and/or vanish into thin air the next. All this those who set down these events in writing, and in particular John, seem to have felt obliged to tell as honestly as they possibly could, with all the many paradoxes and perplexities. To them, they had no alternative. It was simply how it was.

And, however much the cynical, modern mind may try to dismiss the sightings—and the auditory and tactile experiences that accompanied them—as collective hallucinations on the part of a few simple fishermen, history does not allow any such simple verdict. As we have already seen, before Jesus' crucifixion his disciples had not been anything remotely of heroic disposition. At the time of the arrest in Gethsemane most of them had run away. At Caiaphas's house Simon Peter had lied three times, rather than admit to his being one of Jesus's followers, let alone being their Jesus-appointed leader. During the crucifixion on Golgotha, only John had dared show his face anywhere near the cross. And not one of these individuals, even though Jesus had handpicked them as his key disciples, had offered to take charge of his body as it hung dead and useless, after crucifixion and the centurion's lance had done their worst.

Yet, the lesson of history is that there was something so indescribably *real* about the way that the resurrected Jesus presented himself to this altogether unlikely bunch of individuals that their whole personalities became radically and irrevocably transformed, quite literally from the moment of those sightings on. At the very next, major Jewish celebration, Pentecost, a feast that occurs just fifty days after the Passover, the previously timid and backsliding Simon Peter told a huge Jerusalem crowd about what he and his companions had experienced with such spirit and conviction that that very same day three thousand people reportedly became "Christians" (Acts 2:41).

And it was a process that quickly became unstoppable. A few years later Peter had developed the confidence to address even a Roman centurion and an entirely non-Jewish gathering with these forceful words:

You must have heard about the recent happenings in Judaea, about Jesus of Nazareth and how he . . .

went about doing good and curing. . . . Now, I and those with me can witness to everything he did throughout the countryside of Judaea and in Jerusalem itself; and also to the fact that they killed him by hanging him on a tree. Yet three days afterwards God raised him to life and allowed him to be seen, not by the whole people, but only by certain witnesses. Now we are those witnesses. We have eaten and drunk with him after his resurrection from the dead. He has ordered us to proclaim this to his people . . . that all who believe in Jesus will have their sins forgiven through his name. (Acts 10:37–43)

Simon Peter and the other followers, now clearly convinced that death was never the end of *their* lives, went out and about, fearlessly preaching what Jesus had taught them, and describing the events of Golgotha in this way. In this same cause they not only declared their preparedness to risk a fate every bit as dire as Jesus'—they positively demonstrated this preparedness by accepting whatever fate came their way with an equanimity that won them and their cause more and more converts. Peter himself was crucified, reputedly asking to undergo this upside down. And in the course of the next three centuries thousands of Christians similarly died as martyrs in Roman arenas, only for still more to come forward, seemingly out of nowhere, to take their place. It was a process that against all odds established the world religion that is Christianity today.

Even so, there can be no absolute certainties about those strange sightings associated with a Jesus who had seemed so very dead when crucified on Golgotha and who was buried just a stone's throw away. This is not, however, to excuse some of the more unworthy speculations that have arisen, particularly in our own proof-demanding era. For some decades now there has been a highly popular vogue to explain away Jesus' "resurrection" as simply a physical resuscitation following which Jesus slipped away to southern France to live happily ever after with Mary of Magdala. *Holy Blood, Holy Grail* and *The Da Vinci Code* are but two examples. "Late and quite unfounded" are the words which the *Oxford Dictionary of the Christian Church* used as long ago as 1957 to dismiss the flimsy ninth-century legend upon which some beguiling modern-day variants of this story have been based. If the southern France legend were true, then the testimonies of sightings discussed in this chapter, all well documented from at least as early as the second century, would need to be dismissed as so much wastepaper. It is the southern France legend, not the four testimonies, that is unfounded. And the very idea that Jesus should have wandered off to a Provençal retirement, cynically letting his followers die for him in their thousands back in the rest of the Roman world is an affront both to the basic integrity of our four testimony writers, and to all that can be understood of the human Jesus himself.

But of course, even after all the investigative approaches that we have tried in this book, there can still be no scientific proof that the circumstances of Jesus' death

22—Where hundreds of followers of Jesus died for their beliefs. The famous Colosseum of Rome, just one of the many Roman entertainment centers where Christians might be mauled by lions or set alight as spectacles for public amusement. As the Roman historian Tacitus described the emperor Nero's persecution of Christians living within a generation of Jesus' lifetime: "Their deaths were made farcical. Dressed in wild animal skins, they were torn to pieces like dogs, or crucified, or made into torches to be ignited after dark as substitutes for daylight." Nero presented such spectacles in Rome's Gardens shortly before a later emperor built the Colosseum. The inset is from a relief on a Roman terracotta lamp of the first century A.D. showing a hapless victim being mauled by lions.

and return to life really were as our testimony writers have described. Even so, as we are just about to see, there are some interesting ways by which our Golgotha crime investigation file can and should remain ever active.

16

Can We Ever
Close the File?

✝

THROUGHOUT THIS CRIME SCENE INVESTIGA-
tion we have needed to draw much information from the
four testimonies witnessing to the events of Golgotha.
Yet, we have also found them in certain details to be
flawed by differences between one version and another.
So why should we take any of them seriously?

As we all know, gold rarely exists as pure nuggets. It
needs to be painstakingly extracted from baser materials.
In much the same way, probably not one of our four testimonies consists of pure eyewitness testimony from start
to finish. Instead, each testimony has *some* pure material
as from someone who may well have been a direct eyewitness. But this material has sometimes been edited, and
mixed together with material of lower-grade value, by
slightly later individuals who were writing at second-
hand, and were each trying to provide a more comprehen-

sive account for their own local communities of recent converts.

A typical case in point is the Matthew testimony. As theologians of all denominations have long agreed, this cannot have been written in its entirety by the Matthew referred to in the testimonies as a tax-collector disciple of Jesus (Matthew 9:9). This is because the Matthew testimony shows a lot of influence from that of Mark, of whose author there has never been any tradition identifying him as an immediate disciple of Jesus. So why should one of the "Twelve," who had traveled around with Jesus repeatedly, have deferred to an individual of lesser direct experience? As we have already seen, the Matthew testimony reported earthquakes at the moment of Jesus' death on Golgotha and at the time of his resurrection in the tomb. The fact that no one else reported such unmissable happenings gives us cause for considerable skepticism towards at least this part of the Matthew testimony.

On the other hand, the Matthew testimony has probably the best verbatim assemblage of Jesus' teachings and parables of any of the four. It is also the most Jewish, with many references to contemporary Jewish customs. All of which neatly equates with a very early tradition, dating no later than A.D. 130, that Matthew the tax collector had "compiled the sayings of Jesus in the Aramaic language, and everyone translated them as well as they could." In other words, some unknown, later editor, "Matthew," took the true tax collector Matthew's original document, translated it into Greek, then embellished it throughout with narrative material following much the same semihistorical formula that Mark had adopted.

Though very likely it was this same later editor, "Matthew," who waxed a little too fanciful on matters such as the earthquakes, even he had his own important contribution to make. For in his telling the story of the Temple guards posted to watch over Jesus' tomb, and how they had fled at the time of Jesus' resurrection, he went on with a point given in no other testimony:

> Some of the guards went off into the city to tell the chief priests all that had happened. These . . . handed a considerable sum of money to the soldiers with these instructions: "This is what you must say, 'His disciples came during the night and stole him away while we were asleep.' And should the governor [i.e., Pilate] come to hear of this, we undertake to put things right with him ourselves and to see that you do not get into trouble." So they took the money, and to this day that is the story among the Jews. (Matthew 28:11–15)

The interesting aspect of this passage is that for the Temple priesthood to have wanted it put out, even as a lie, that Jesus' disciples had stolen his body from the tomb, in itself constitutes an admission that Jesus' body *did* vanish in some rather mysterious way. And there is a further intriguing inference. This is that, if we can believe that Temple guards were indeed posted outside Jesus' tomb during that crucial thirty-six hours after the crucifixion, then they might actually have been the first and the nearest witnesses of whatever had occurred when Jesus' body underwent its resurrection inside.

For what was it that these guards told their employers, the Temple chief priests, of what had really happened, that the latter preferred to pay a "considerable sum of money," rather than allow this to be circulated? Had the guards, in the early hours of the Sunday morning, seen some unearthly light or heard some strange noise inside the tomb, and pushed aside the entrance boulder (as they had the manpower to do), only to find the body inside inexplicably vanished? This would actually explain what has never otherwise been explained—that is, how and why the large tomb entrance boulder should have been found already moved when the women arrived. This, even though Jesus himself, who repeatedly demonstrated his resurrected body's ability to pass through closed doors, clearly had no need to move this.

In the case of the Mark testimony, the general thinking is that the writing of this version preceded those of Matthew and Luke. Both of these latter show some dependence on it. And it tells its stories in simpler, less elaborate, and thereby arguably more original forms than they do. Some scholars have hypothesized that Mark may have been the young man who fled naked when his *sindon* was grabbed by the Temple guards at the time of Jesus' arrest. This is because Mark's is the only testimony to mention this incident. If this were the case, then he may actually have been a close observer of some of the key events in his own right.

The more widely accepted view of Mark, deriving from the same pre–A.D. 130 authority responsible for the information about Matthew, is that he was some kind of secretary or interpreter to Simon Peter. As "John Mark," he would later be described as setting out with St. Paul on the first of the latter's missionary journeys (Acts 12:25; 13:13; 15:37). Mark's testimony thereby carries some potentially first-hand information, but otherwise a lot of very high-grade, secondhand recording of events.

Still, with regard to Mark, his testimony provides an interesting instance of what could happen to the actual documents of these testimonies during their earliest and most vulnerable years. Two of the world's oldest full Bibles, both dating from the late fourth century, are the Codex Vaticanus in Rome, and the Codex Sinaiticus in London's British Museum, the latter housed for many centuries in the remote St. Catherine's monastery in Egypt's Sinai desert. Both of these Bibles, written in Greek, incorporate Mark's gospel, along with the other three. However, they have missing from their texts the last eleven verses of the last chapter in Mark, as found in the Bibles that we use today. In a preprinting age in which everything was hand copied, it would appear that a back page of a very early original Mark manuscript became detached, or abraded away, leaving the book's ending missing. A vital ending, because it may have borne some lost information about Jesus' post-resurrection appearances, perhaps concerning that mysterious "first" one to Simon Peter. Though someone supplied as an ending the final eleven verses that appear in our present Bibles, there is a strong likelihood that these were not the Mark author's own original words.

Probably the closest and the most reliable eyewitness descriptions of the events surrounding the Gethsemane crime scene are those in the John testimony, a source that ironically was once supposed to be the latest and the least reliable of the four. By any standards, John's is a strange piece of work compared with the other three. While Matthew, Mark, and Luke include a lot of narrative along with teachings and parables in the early part of their testimonies, John fills the equivalent part mostly with long, highly theological discourses by Jesus. But when it comes to the actual events surrounding our Golgotha crime scene, no one is more graphic or more insistently an eyewitness than John. It is John who describes the lance producing blood and water from Jesus' side, pointing out that "this is the evidence of one who saw it—true evidence, and he knows that what he says is true—and he gives it so that you may believe as well" (John 19:35). It is John who describes the linens left lying in the tomb as the cause for his and Peter's own immediate, on-the-spot belief that Jesus really had come back from the dead (John 20:9).

It is natural to suppose that everything that could ever be deduced concerning what the four testimonies have to say about the Golgotha crime scene must have already been written many times over. It may be a surprise, therefore, that our present, evermore high-tech age is promising to shed its own unique new light on these ancient documents—quite literally. As earlier noted, over a hundred years ago archaeologists working in ancient Egypt began finding fragments of papyri they identified as being from very early copies of the testimonies. Some of these are in the University of Michigan and Princeton University libraries in the United States. Others are in the Chester Beatty collection, Dublin, Ireland. Yet others are at Oxford and Manchester in England. Because these fragments have almost invariably been recovered from ancient trash heaps, for every item which it has been possible to read, there have remained others that up until now scholars have had to set to one side as too stained or otherwise too darkened by time to be legible.

But now, thanks to the latest techniques in digital imaging, a few clicks of a computer mouse can enable a suitably scanned papyrus scrap to be studied in any number of different light variations. This can make ink lettering that has been invisible to the naked eye for perhaps seventeen or eighteen centuries become magically legible once more. Such developments already promise that it may be possible to read some 20 percent more papyrus fragments than have been legible hitherto. So, as these hitherto too dark scraps from the ancient trash heaps begin to be systematically reexamined and deciphered, who knows what future discoveries pertinent to our crime scene may come to light?

Nor are the possibilities of exciting future findings confined just to the written testimonies. One of the most neglected fields of investigation surrounding the Golgotha crime scene concerns what can have happened to the contents of Jesus' tomb immediately following the discovery that his body was missing, and before Emperor Hadrian had topped the spot with a temple of Venus a hundred years later. For it was from the very instant that Peter and "John," gazing upon the discarded linen wrappings, "saw and believed" that the religion called Christianity was born. That very same moment, that dark rock tomb, where a man who had seemed to be mortal demonstrated his defeat of death, logically became the newborn

Christianity's central and most sacred shrine.

So, what happened to the tomb, to the wrappings, and to any other of the tomb's contents in the immediate aftermath of the discoveries made, and the sightings seen, that first Easter Sunday day? We know that Joseph of Arimathea had originally intended the tomb as a brand-new construction for his own personal usage. So now that it was once again without any occupant, did he simply continue with his original plan to have himself buried within it? Did he perhaps have himself laid on the very same ledge on which Jesus' body had been laid, with his bones later gathered up into an ossuary and stored in a niche off the main chamber? Did the tomb become the family vault for other members of his kith and kin?

Although the history of the tomb between the first Easter Sunday and A.D. 135 is a complete blank, all these possibilities seem rather unlikely. Christian tradition carries not the slightest suggestion that Joseph took the tomb back for his own usage. It also attributes other locations nearby as being tombs of both Joseph and of Nicodemus.

So, was Jesus' empty tomb almost immediately accorded the status of the new-born Christianity's foremost shrine? In support of this, there can be no doubt that Jerusalem's earliest known Judeo-Christian synagogue, constructed after A.D. 70 from blocks of the destroyed Temple, was oriented towards it—immediately raising the question, in what manner might Jerusalem's first Christians have maintained it? Did they carry out some structural alterations, as Emperor Constantine would do three hundred years later? Or did they opt to leave it and everything left inside much as Peter and John found it on that first Easter Sunday morning?

While there is no known evidence to suggest that any construction work was carried out, some thought certainly seems to have been given to what to leave inside. Unlike the ancient Egyptians and other pagan peoples, the Jews had no tradition of furnishing their tombs with everyday items as homes for the dead. Nonetheless, given that Jesus' blood would have been splashed on a number of items associated with his last hours of suffering, there could well have been a concern to collect those items together if at all possible, with the otherwise empty tomb their most logical housing.

The linen wrappings that had been around Jesus' body we know to have been in the tomb already. Besides these, the crown of thorns, the nails that had pierced his hands and feet, the crossbeam to which he was nailed, and the "King of the Jews" placard could all have been considered worthy items. In the case of the nails, Joseph of Arimathea and Nicodemus would have automatically acquired these upon their unfastening Jesus' body from the cross. The crown of thorns may well have been immediately at hand for them after they removed it from Jesus' head before en-Shrouding him. In the case of the crossbeam, although theoretically this would have been Roman property, intended to be used again for the next crucifixion victim, a few coins quietly slipped to a Roman centurion may well have secured it for the tomb collection.

And for such items to have been assembled in the manner of a shrine would actually make a lot of sense from what we know—albeit all too little—of the tomb's rediscovery by Empress Helena in A.D. 326. Unsatisfactory as are the fourth-century historical descriptions of this event, they at least sufficiently convey that the tomb chamber contained crucifixion nails, some lengths of wood, as if from a cross or crosses, and, quite specifically, "the board . . . on which Pilate had placed an inscription written in Greek, Latin, and Hebrew." Though no full-length Shroud is mentioned among these items, this latter could well have been removed as unsuitable for storage in the tomb sometime before the tomb had to be hurriedly abandoned upon the expulsion of all Jews from Jerusalem in A.D. 135. If the present-day Turin Shroud is indeed that same cloth, and if my own reconstruction of its history has any validity, then there is some good documentary evidence that it was not left in the tomb with the other objects, but transported to what is today Turkey at a very early stage. There it spent nearly a thousand years in the town known today as Urfa before being transferred to Constantinople, then via French crusaders, to Western Europe.

So, today we have in Turin a Shroud that, despite the adverse findings of the carbon-dating test carried out in 1988, carries some compelling though still inconclusive signs that it was the true, original cloth that lay on that Jerusalem tomb ledge on the first Easter Sunday. We have in Rome a placard bearing the words "Jesus the Nazarene, King of the Jews" that bears compelling, though still inconclusive signs that it was the true, original notice on Jesus' cross, as found by Empress Helena when she rediscovered the Jerusalem tomb in A.D. 326.

And we have in Jerusalem, within the Church of the Holy Sepulchre, what appears to be that true tomb site, albeit that the original rock is all but inaccessible because of the successive ornamental shrines that have been built over it.

All raising the question, might Turin's Shroud and Rome's placard still bear traces on their surfaces of their once intimate association with that tomb in Jerusalem? In which case, might the latest modern-day crime scene investigation methods actually be able to show this onetime close association in much the same manner that certain varieties of dust on a suspect's clothing can connect him to a particular crime scene?

Readily suggesting that this might be possible is the fact that the original rock of the Jerusalem tomb, though so difficult to access because of all the overlying shrines, can almost certainly be determined as limestone. Limestone is the main rock on which all of Jerusalem is built. And limestone has an interesting property. Every different bed of it exhibits slight differences in its crystalline structure from the next bed, just as human beings have different fingerprints from each other. Ion microprobes can analyze tiny specks of limestone dust and show clearly which may have come from the same bed and which are from perhaps thousands of miles away.

Equally suggesting the possibility of some such association is the fact that as recently as 2003 the Shroud's underside—the side that would have lain in direct contact with the tomb's limestone ledge—was temporarily exposed for the first time in four and a half centuries. This occurred when Swiss conservator Dr. Mechthild Flury-

Lemberg removed the Shroud's sixteenth-century backing cloth as part of a major conservation program. Large quantities of microscopic debris were retrieved from the cloth's underside in the course of this conservation work, much of which has yet to be analyzed properly. However, the likelihood of it containing limestone dust is undoubtedly high, as evident from preliminary studies by an earlier investigator, Turin's Professor Giovanni Riggi. In 1978 Riggi found some significant quantities of limestone dust when just a small section of the Shroud's underside was unstitched.

Currently, therefore, there exists the tantalizing prospect that whenever the shrines covering Jesus' tomb become dismantled for repair work, thereby exposing its original limestone bedrock, scientific comparison between this limestone and that found adhering to the Turin Shroud's underside will become possible. And while no one has hitherto considered extending such a study also to include the Church of Santa Croce in Gerusalemme's "King of the Jews" placard, it would be fascinating if this too were found to bear some similarly matching limestone dust.

Of course there is no guarantee that any such sampling work will produce evidence of a match. Nor, in the event of there being no match, should either the tomb site, the Shroud, or the placard necessarily be dismissed as inauthentic solely for such a reason. The Shroud may be authentic, the tomb site not. Or vice versa. Or the original ledge of the tomb may have been of a different stone from the bedrock, a stone removed long ago when Moslems made determined attempts to destroy the entire site.

Ultimately what can only be concluded, with complete confidence, is that the file on our Golgotha crime scene is very far from closed, and it is unlikely ever to be. At the heart of whatever happened on Golgotha there lies not only the world's greatest murder mystery, but also its greatest religious mystery. That is, that a man who was most brutally and most publicly killed at that spot two thousand years ago could, and arguably did, come back from death within thirty-six hours, just as he predicted he would.

It is highly unlikely that there will ever be some forensic test or tests by which any crime scene investigator will be able to fathom entirely what happened, given the very nature of those events. As one Jewish-born Shroud investigator, the late Dr. Alan Adler, often remarked, "There is no test for Christness."

However, in their seeking answers to the mysteries of Golgotha, science and religion rightly converge as one. These are mysteries on which their files, along with our minds, can and should remain forever open.

Select Bibliography

✠

Barbet, Pierre. *A Doctor at Calvary*. New York: Image Books, 1963.

Biddle, Martin. *The Tomb of Christ*. Stroud, Gloucestershire, England: Sutton, 1999.

Garza-Valdes, Leoncio. *The DNA of God*. New York: Doubleday, 1999.

Greenhut, Z. "Burial Cave of the Caiaphas Family." *Biblical Archaeology Review*, 18, 5, Sept/Oct 1992, pp. 29 ff.

Haas, Nicu. "Anthropological Observations on the Skeletal Remains from Giv'at ha-Mivtar." *Israel Exploration Journal*, vol 20, nos 1–2, 1970.

Hesemann, Michael. *Die stummen Zeugen von Golgatha: Die faszinierende Geschichte der Passionreliquien Christi*, Munich: Hugendubel, 2000.

Josephus. *The Jewish War*, trans. G. A. Williamson, revised E. Mary Smallwood. Harmondsworth: Penguin, 1981.

————. *The Antiquities of the Jews,* trans. H. Thackeray. London: Loeb Classsical Library, 6 vols., 1930–1965.

Metzger, Bruce. *Manuscripts of the Greek Bible, an Introduction to Palaeography,* Oxford University Press, 1981.

Morison, Frank. *Who Moved the Stone?* London: Faber & Faber, n.d.

Nitowski, Eugenia Louise. *Reconstructing the Tomb of Christ from Archaeological and Literary Sources,* Ph.D. dissertation for the University of Notre Dame, Indiana, 1979.

Pixner, Bargil. "Church of the Apostles found on Mount Zion," *Biblical Archaeology Review,* 16, 3, May/June 1990, pp. 16 ff.

Prag, Kay. *Blue Guide, Jerusalem.* London: A. & C. Black and New York: W. W. Norton, 1989.

Ritmeyer, Kathleen, and Leen. "Reconstructing Herod's Temple Mount in Jerusalem," *Biblical Archaeology Review* 15, 6, Nov/Dec 1989, pp. 23 ff.

Robinson, John A. T. *Can We Trust the New Testament?* London: Mowbray, 1977.

Schmoger, Carl E. *The Life of Jesus Christ and Biblical Revelations, from the Visions of the Venerable Anne Catherine Emmerich, as Recorded in the Journals of Clemens Brentano.* Rockford, Ill.: Tan Books, 1979.

Schonfield, Hugh J. *The Passover Plot.* London: Hutchinson, 1965.

Taylor, Joan. "The Garden of Gethsemane: Not the place of Jesus' Arrest." *Biblical Archaeology Review,* 21, 4, July/August 1995, pp. 26ff.

Thiede, Carsten, and Matthew d'Ancona. *The Quest for the True Cross*. New York: Palgrave, 2002.

Vermes, Geza. *Jesus the Jew*. London: Collins, 1973.

Wilson, Ian. *The Shroud of Turin*. New York: Doubleday, 1978.

———. *Jesus: The Evidence*. London: Weidenfeld & Nicolson, 1994.

———. *The Blood and the Shroud*. London: Orion, 1998.

Zugibe, Frederick Y. *The Crucifixion of Jesus: A Forensic Inquiry*. New York: M. Evans, 2005.